Ancient Indian Scientific Thought and Modern Theories

Samīkṣikā - 14

General Editor
Pratapanand Jha

The Samīkṣikā Series is aimed at compiling the research papers presented by the distinguished scholars and specialists in the seminars organized by the National Mission for Manuscripts. The seminars provide an interactive forum for scholars to present to a large audience, ideas related to the knowledge contained in India's textual heritage.

Ancient Indian Scientific Thought and Modern Theories

– An Overview –

Editors

Dhirendranath Banerjee

Sanjit Kumar Sadhukhan

राष्ट्रीय पाण्डुलिपि मिशन

॥ विज्ञानमुपास्व ॥

National Mission for Manuscripts

DK PRINTWORLD

Publishers of Indian Traditions

Cataloging in Publication Data — DK
[Courtesy: D.K. Agencies (P) Ltd. <docinfo@dkagencies.com>]

Seminar - Ancient Indian Scientific Thought vis-à-vis Modern Scientific Theories, Discoveries and Development (2017 : Kolkata, India)
Ancient Indian scientific thought and modern theories : an overview / editors, Dhirendranath Banerjee, Sanjit Kumar Sadhukhan.
pages cm (Samīkṣikā; no. 14)
"... proceedings of a three-day Seminar – Ancient Indian Scientific Thought vis-à-vis Modern Scientific Theories, Discoveries and Development – held during 25-27 March 2017 in Kolkata, organized by the Sanskrit Sahitya Parishad, Kolkata, and sponsored by the National Mission for Manuscripts" – Foreword.

1. Science – India – History – Congresses. 2. Science, Ancient Congresses. I. Banerjee, Dhirendranath, editor. II. Sadhukhan, Sanjit Kumar, editor. III. Sanskrit Sahitya Parishat (Kolkata, India), organizer. IV. National Mission for Manuscripts (India), sponsoring body, publisher. V. Title.

LCC Q127.I4S46 2017 | DDC 509.54 23

Papers presented at a national seminar on "Ancient Indian Scientific Thought vis-à-vis Modern Scientific Theories: Discoveries and Development", held at Sanskrit Sahitya Parishad, Kolkata, during 25-27 March 2017.

ISBN: 978-81-904029-6-5 (Samīkṣikā Series)
ISBN: 978-93-80829-66-1 (Hardbound)
First published in India in 2019

Published by:
National Mission for Manuscripts
11, Mansingh Road, New Delhi - 110001
Phone: (011) 2338 3894; Fax: 2307 3340
e-mail: director.namami@nic.in
Website: www.namami.nic.in

Co-published by:
D.K. Printworld (P) Ltd.
Regd. Office: "Vedaśrī", F-395, Sudarshan Park
(Metro Station: ESI Hospital), New Delhi - 110015
Phones: (011) 2545 3975; 2546 6019; Fax: (011) 2546 5926
e-mail: indology@dkprintworld.com
Website: www.dkprintworld.com

Printed by: D.K. Printworld (P) Ltd., New Delhi

Foreword

THE National Mission for Manuscripts (NMM), New Delhi, is making an untiring effort to retrieve hidden literary treasures across different disciplines and making serious attempts to disseminate such knowledge for the benefit of the entire world. Through seminars and conferences, the seed of the concepts takes the shape of a tree, before it is taken for publication.

The volume in hand is the proceedings of a three-day seminar – Ancient Indian Scientific Thought vis-à-vis Modern Scientific Theories, Discoveries and Development – held during 25-27 March 2017 in Kolkata, organized by the Sanskrit Sahitya Parishad, Kolkata, and sponsored by the National Mission for Manuscripts.

The Western misconception is that India lacked in scientific advancements in her past, and her literature provides no or very little clues to substantiate her claim of scientific and technological discoveries. This in spite of the sincere efforts of some well-known Western scholars like Sir William Jones, Albert Einstine and Frits Staal heighlighting India's significant contributions in the development of science and technology, especially with her contribution of zero, and foothold on astrology, astronomy, Āyurveda, chemistry, natural sciences, physics, surgery, and so on.

The National Mission for Manuscripts is pleased to present this volume as it bears testimony to the fact that Indian sages, philosophers and scholars had a grip on all the topics that the modern-day scientists deal with, including complicated surgery and quantum physics. Our Vedas, Upaniṣads and other literary works were the storehouse of scientific wisdom, though the prevailing socio-religious conditions of the past impeded its widespread dissemination. It is my hope that the topics discussed here will pave the way for further researches that will unearth India's hidden ancient wisdom and knowhow.

Pratapanand Jha
Director
National Mission for Manuscripts

Contents

Introduction

Dhirendranath Banerjee
and
Sanjit Kumar Sadhukhan

THIS volume, the proceedings of a three-day seminar "Ancient Indian Scientific Thought vis-à-vis Modern Scientific Theories, Discoveries and Development" held in Kolkata during 25-27 March 2017 contains nine scholarly papers, including the Inaugural Address of Prof. Dilip Kumar Mohanta, the first Vice-Chancellor of the Sanskrit College and University, Kolkata.

Prof. Mohanta, in his Inaugural Address, makes one revisit the development of Indian science and technology in varied fields since the Vedic period and suggests that we have a living tradition which is very dynamic in nature, inheriting at the same time claiming freedom from the past. Our understanding of heritage needs to be philosophical. Knowing is an ever-enlarging arena, which is subject to change and modification. No word is final and sacrosanct in the realm of knowledge; it is always open-ended. One has no adequate reason to believe in any qualitative difference between scientific pursuit and philosophical pursuit. Inheritance is to be analysed, modified, corrected and made alive with fresh thinking and vitality of the age.

In his paper, "Scientific Thoughts in Indian Philosophy", Sanjit Kumar Sadhukhan states that it is absurd to think that the literature of India is totally devoid of scientific phenomena, thoughts or results. The Indian poetical and philosophic works provide enough details about the development of science and technology in ancient India. One gets to know of the enough discussions of there in the Vaiśeṣika and Yoga schools of Indian philosophy.

While the former deals with such concepts like *dravya* (substance), *guṇa* (quality), and *karma* (motion) and the cause of different types of motion, the latter talks about the *yoga* and its health benefits. The physical postures and meditative practices of *yoga* actually developed through thousands of years of intensive study of the body's responses to particular postures and meditations. The modern world approves of its benefits in health management.

Dhirendranath Banerjee, in his paper "Ancient Indian Cosmology vis-à-vis Modern Scientific Cosmology" makes a detailed analysis of both the ancient and modern cosmologies. He delves deep into the Indian philosophical systems, especially Samkhya, Nyāya–Vaiśeṣika, Mīmāṁsā and Vedānta, along with the Buddhist and Jaina philosophies, and brings forth the varied theories of creation, concepts of time and atom. He presents a detailed classification of the theories of cosmology under different headings like philosophy, religion and modern scientific developments. The cosmological understanding of the Babylonians, Greeks, Romans, Chinese and Christians is also featured. From the scientific point of view, the paper deals with Pythagoras' theory of cosmology, geocentric theory of Aristotle, Ptolemy, Claudius Ptolemicus, Nicolaus Copnicus, Tycho Brahe, Johanese Kepler, Galileo Galilee and Isaac Newton.

Surgical study on corpses and empirical methodology of the Cārvākas/Lokāyatas were decried in the Dharmaśātras. To save their science, even doctors had to pay lip service to orthodoxy. Same was the case with astronomers as they had to submit to the Vedic view on the causes of the solar and lunar eclipses. Āryabhata was misinterpreted for his geokinetic hypothesis, against the then current geostatic view, and of late *Āryabhaṭīya* was tampered. Orthodoxy did severely affect the growth of science from the academic point of view. This is the limelight of Ramkrishna Bhattacharya's paper "Scientific Outlook in Ancient Academic Tradition".

In "The Concept of Matter: A Philosophy–Physics Interface" Raghunath Ghosh concentrates on the concept of matter in Indian tradition and its dynamic character. There is an eternal dispute between the spiritualists and the materialists for supremacy. There are varying approaches to physics, especially matter, in Indian philosophical systems. Sri Aurobindo respects the claims of both. According to him, matter is nothing but the non-manifested *sat*-element of the spirit called *Satchidānanda*. The paper discusses about the views of many a scholar on the concept and the views of those who deal with Quantum Physics.

Zero is the greatest gift of India to the world. Without it the present prosperity of modern civilizations through various scientific achievements would not have been possible. In his paper "Zero: An Eternal Enigma", Parthasarathi Mukhopadhyay talks about the genesis of zero and its application among some of the oldest civilizations of the world such as Egyptian, Babylonian (Akkadian), Mexican (Maya), Peruvian (Inca), Chinese, Greek and Roman. It makes one travel through the Egyptian hieroglyphics, via Babylonian clay tablets and grotesque-looking Mayan glyphs, the ingenious Inca *quipu*, and the great Greek civilization and mighty Roman Empire.

Amalendu Bandhyopadhyay in his paper "Astrology versus Astronomy" discusses the relation between both the sciences. Astrology is indeed a part of astronomy. Recently astrology has made fast inroads into the minds of the Indian people. Astrology is based on the classical concept of earth-centric universe, while astronomy is solar-centric. There is thus a fundamental difference. Horoscopes are prepared based on the astrological calculations and many a time such predictions fail. Most of the astrological predictions on natural calamities have failed.

Jagapati Sarkar in "The Asiatic Society and the Initiation of History of Science" deals with the quintessential role that the Asiatic Society played in propagating the literary, cultural and scientific enquiries of ancient India. By its firm focus, the Society has become the cultural focus of the country. The paper discusses the role of Sir William Jones in building the Society up and enlarging the focus from languages, literature and culture to natural sciences, of late. It takes one through the dedicated efforts of the Society and its published works.

Manuscripts on astronomy, especially those in Sanskrit, are basic historical evidences which can stand as a proof of our history. There are hundreds of such manuscripts preserved in Oriental libraries. Somenath Chatterjee takes us to many such storehouses through "Ninth Century Onwards Astronomical Manuscripts in Oriental Libraries of India". Traditionally the local rulers and the rich men were the collectors of these manuscripts. However, of late, there were efforts to collect, catalogue and preserve them in the Oriental libraries.

Inaugural Address

Freedom in Ideas

Dilip Kumar Mohanta

RESPECTED Chairman of this inaugural Session Professor Sadhan Chandra Sarkar, the Secretary of the Sanskrita Sahitya Parishad, Professor Dhirendranath Banerjee, distinguished scholars and professors on the dais, respected members of the Executive Committee of Sanskrita Sahitya Parishad, guests and friends, I feel proud and privileged as being invited here to inaugurate the Three-Day National Seminar on "Ancient Indian Scientific Thought vis-à-vis Modern Scientific Theories, Discoveries and Development", sponsored by National Mission for Manuscripts, New Delhi. I congratulate both the organizer and the sponsor for making it possible here in Kolkata at this Heritage Institution of Indological Studies. Today we may take effort to revive the Indological studies not only for inspiring our youths about our glorious past but also for new lights on some of our modern issues. We understand that a scientific enquiry must proceed in an orderly manner, adopting only those procedures that are trustworthy, and subject to verification and correction. In ancient times Indians were pioneers in Mathematics, Chemistry, Physiology, Plant and Consciousness Studies, Origin of Life, Medicine, etc.

We know that Acharya Prafulla Chandra Roy's *Hindu Chemistry* (vol. 2) contains an appendix. It contains an introduction by Acharya Brojendra Nath Seal. This later on became the concluding chapter of his magnum opus *The Positive Sciences of the Ancient Hindus* (*TPSH*). There he deals with the various scientific methods that were developed and employed by the Hindus in their scientific works and in their philosophical analysis.

Seal observes:

> Philosophy in its rise and development is necessarily governed by the body of positive knowledge preceding or accompanying it. Hindu philosophy *on its empirical side* was dominated by concepts derived from physiology and philology, just as Greek Philosophy was similarly dominated by geometrical concepts and methods . . . criticism and estimate of Hindu thought must take note of the empirical basis on which the speculative superstructure was raised. – *TPSH*: iv

The progress of Indian Algebra (mainly in southern India) after Bhaskara, parallel to the developments in China and Japan, is the subject that remains for future investigation.

In today's academic activities – either in philosophy or in the history of science in India – the Hindu's inductive method or methods of algebraic analysis and scientific ideas:

> ... have deeply influenced the course of natural philosophy in Asia – in the East as well as the West – in China and Japan; as well as in the Saracen Empire. A comparative estimate of Greek and Hindu science may now be undertaken with some measure of success and finality. – Ibid.: vi

This observation is extremely important today because of the claim motivated by the biased effort to prove the religious customs of Hindus with the help of scientific explanations. There is much enthusiasm to claim that all the recent discoveries and inventions in science were known to the Hindus from the Vedic age onwards. On the other hand, there is another extreme claim that Hindu civilization is basically mystical and there is no sign of scientific and rational thinking. In the midst of this extremely perplexing situation, rereading and researching of ancient Indian scientific thought and its comparison to the development of modern science are important. Because this interdisciplinary study of ancient science of India might allow us to get rid of the exclusive and absolute claims and also enable us to see where we are correct and where we are wrong. Keeping parity with the open-endedness and flexibility in learning as visualized by the Vedic seers, "let noble thought come to us from different directions" (*ā no bhadrā kratavo yantu viśvataḥ* – *R̥gveda* I.89.101) and in spite of being admirers of Sanskrit, we should not be "orthodox" in our attitude and should not live within the boundary of the past as wrongly understood and argued by some "ill-informed" scholars of Indology. What is old is not necessarily good and what is new is also not necessarily bad. The greatest bondage is the slavery of thought, and therefore, for our betterment we are to enjoy freedom in ideas. As cautioned by Kālidāsa:

पुराणमित्येव न साधु सर्वं न चापि काव्यं नवमित्यवद्यम्।
सन्तः परीक्ष्यान्यतरद्भजन्ते मूढः परप्रत्ययनेयबुद्धिः॥

purāṇamityeva na sādhu sarvaṁ na cāpi kāvyaṁ navamityavadyam ।
santaḥ parīkṣyānyataradbhajante muḍhaḥ parapratyayaneyabuddhiḥ ॥

This attitude makes us free from our total and blind obedience to scriptures (Śāstra). By the word "tradition" I do not mean the sense of "orthodoxy". There cannot be a system of living philosophy if it is confined to "orthodoxy". "Orthodoxy" suggests a lifeless, finalized structure. But a living tradition, as we see in Indian philosophical heritage, is always dynamic; it inherits the past as well as claims freedom from the past. Through interpretation and reinterpretation in view of the changing and new contextual development of ideas we can keep our philosophical tradition alive. Our understanding of heritage is desired to be philosophical in the sense that it upholds the view, "straight is the way, narrow is the lane that leadth unto truth". Our understanding is to be guided by the attitude of "traditional–modernity"or to use Martin Heidegger's phrase "distancing nearness in the sense in which we inherit the past as well as we claim freedom from the past". I am sure in the forthcoming different academic sessions there will be Paṇḍita-vāda (scholarly debate) on different dimensions of the main theme of the National Seminar. Because, the arena of knowing is ever-enlarging and it is always subject to change and modification. There cannot be any final and sacrosanct word in the realm of knowledge; it is always open-ended. So unfinalizability always characterizes our scientific and philosophic enterprise in the context of knowledge. And whatever number of value we assign to our explanation of the nature of the world, it is not the final explanation. We cannot ignore the knowledge of science and history of our time. I do not see any adequate reason to believe in any qualitative difference between scientific pursuit and philosophic pursuit. It is possible to have a bridge between the information and insight provided by scientific discoveries and philosophic adventures of thought.

But before concluding my speech I wish to quote philosopher Bimal Krishna Matilal. What Matilal in the concluding part of an essay titled दर्शनचर्चा ओ भारतीय महिला has written in Bengali is important for us today for doing philosophy in a meaningful way:

> आमार मने हय सृजनशील दार्शनिक चिन्तारधारक जन्ये भारतीय सनातनी दर्शनचिन्तार अन्तष्टि ग्रहण करे पाचत्यदर्शनेर आधुनिक धारार विचार-विश्लेषण करा प्रयोजन, ए निये बिभिन्न दिक थेके वितर्के सृष्टिरओ प्रयोजन। तबेइ हबे जीबन्तधारार सृष्टि। आधुनिकाले आमादेर देशे संस्कृतज्ञ पण्डितराओ एखनओ नाना बिचार-बितर्के अंशग्रहण करेन बटे किन्तु तार सङ्गे आधुनिक चिन्ताधाराके मेशाते हबे।
>
> – नीतियुक्तिओधर्म, पृ. १६२, १३९५ बङ्गाब्द

> I think, we need examination of modern trend of thoughts of Western philosophy with inner sight of the thoughts of Indian classical philosophy in order to promote the trend of creative philosophy. There is also a need of initiation of debate from different sides in this regard. Only then, there will be birth of a living trend. In modern times, the Sanskrit *paṇḍit*s participate in various debates, in our country, still now, but there should be a mixing of modern philosophical thoughts with it.

Today inheritance is to be analysed, modified, corrected and made alive with fresh thinking and vitality of the age.

I sincerely thank all those who are either directly or indirectly associated with this seminar. With these few words I inaugurate this National Seminar. I wish success of this seminar. Thank you all once again.

3

Astrology versus Astronomy

Amalendu Bandhyopadhyay

ASTROLOGY is one of most popular of all the fringe areas of science and appears to be gaining in popularity. Since many consider astrology to be a science – indeed a part of astronomy – there is good reason for everyone in the astronomical community to become familiar with the scientific evidence of astrology. The term is most often used to signify a purported science that describes relationship between specific celestial configurations and human affairs. The basic concept of astrology is that the position of the heavenly bodies at the time and place of an individual's birth, influence or is correlated with his or her personality, physical characteristics, health, profession and future destiny. Classical astrology regarded the Earth as the centre of the universe, with the planets, stars, Sun and Moon orbiting around it. The heavenly bodies were originally considered divine and possessing magical characteristics. Thus Mars thought to be of red colour, represented the god of war and signified courage and aggression. Venus was thought to be soft and white and was the goddess of love and beauty.

What does science have to say about astrology? First, modern astronomy has negated its key principle that the Earth is the centre of our solar system. We now know that the planets circle the Sun, that our solar system is on the outskirts of a galaxy, which itself is only a part of an expanding universe which contains millions of galaxies. According to astrology there are nine planets, Sun, Moon, Rahu, Ketu, Mercury, Venus, Mars, Jupiter and Saturn. It is now well known that the Sun and the Moon are not planets. The Sun is a star and the Moon is a satellite. Moreover, Rahu and

Ketu are non-existent, as they are intersection points of the ecliptic and the lunar orbit. Thus out of nine planets which form the very basis of astrology, two are not planets and two do not exist at all.

According to Laplace's theory of solar system formation, our solar system was once a very large gas cloud, extending well beyond the reaches of our present solar system. The gas of this low density nebula would have been initially at a vey high temperature, the temperature being so high as to prevent immediate collapse due to gravitational forces pulling the mass together. As this nebula gradually cooled, Laplace considered that it should begin to contract and that rings of gas would be successively shed by the parent nebula. Laplace then expected that these rings, under their own gravitational influences, would break up into separate condensations and the beginnings of the planets would thus occur. Hence planets were once formed part of the solar nebula, according to science. How such planets which are huge lumps of matter situated millions of kilometers away can be intruders in the affairs of man, boggles one's comprehension. Moreover, it is ridiculous to attribute all kinds of human qualities to planets. According to the theory of astrologers, depending on its positions, a planet can be benevolent, malevolent, friendly, furious, revengeful and so on. It is really unfortunate that the crude and false ideas which entered into the minds of our ignorant ancestors continue to have powerful sway on the mind of man living in this age of science and technology.

The horoscope has astrology as its basis. The horoscope of a person is written depending on the positions of the planets at the time of his birth. According to astrologers, all the landmarks in the life of a person are assumed to be safely deposited in that document. Is it not meaningless to believe that the position of a planet will have a say in educational attainment, profession, marriage, foreign travel, accidents, death and so on? Planets are assumed to play a very important role in matrimonial connections. Before the fixing up of any marriage, the horoscopes of the bride and the bridegroom are critically examined by the astrologer who gives the final green signal. It is a common knowledge that not all marriages performed even after scrupulously matching the horoscopes of the brides and the bridegrooms have been found successful. Such was a case with the famous writer Bankimchandra, author of our national song, "Vande Mataram". The wedding ceremony of the daughter of Bankimchandra was performed after "exceptional matching" of horoscopes by astrologers, but within a very short time after the marriage she became a widow. Thereafter, Bankimchandra lost all his faith in astrology. In this connection, it is very interesting to note that more than 90 per cent of the people in the world do not have horoscopes and their marriages are as happy or unhappy as those of others and as such astrology, not having universal validity, cannot claim the status of science. Moreover, it is a common knowledge that generally no two astrologers agree with each other and it appears as though each has got his own way of forecasting and yet astrology is claimed to be a science.

Again, the critical analysis of natural calamities delivers another mortal blow to astrology. Let us consider the unfortunate victims of a plane crash, an earthquake, a cyclone, a volcanic eruption and so on. Should we come to the conclusion that the horoscopes of all such unfortunate victims tell the same fate for all of them? Certainly this is absurd. It is equally preposterous to believe that all the horoscopes of such natural calamity victims will reveal the same date of death.

One of the most widely held beliefs about lunar effects is that there are many more human births at the time of full moon than at other times of the lunar cycle. The belief is even widespread among nurses in maternity wards and among some gynaecologists as well. George Abell and Benneth Greenspan examined all births, live and dead, from the records of the UCLA Hospital maternity ward in the US, during the period 17 March 1974 to 30 April 1978. Their analysis of the nearly 12,000 live and dead births occurring at the UCLA Hospital in an interval of 51 lunar months from 1974 to 1978 reveals no correlation between the numbers of births and full moon or any other phase of the Moon. The role of the Moon as the principal raiser of tides on the Earth has been known for many hundreds of years and was first explained in terms of gravitational theory by Isaac Newton in the seventeenth century. But several pieces of evidence at hand suggest that many of the incredible claims about the influence of the Moon on man are simply not facts at all.

It may be appropriate to cite that in the field of science, if something goes wrong then a thorough investigation would be made to know the exact causes of the failure so that suitable remedial measures may be taken. This is not done in astrology. Moreover, the sciences provide an internal check on each other. The findings in psychology, for example, are consistent with the findings in other sciences. In the case of astrology, however, its claims run counter to what we know in physics, biology and psychology. Although all scientific theories have some problems, astrology is beset with so many anomalies that only by denying all the other sciences could it continue to stand.

A very important prediction made by astrologers, which was proved to be totally false, may be cited here. Indian astrologers cried hoarse from the roof tops and gave a severe warning to the public that on the occasion of the conjunction of eight planets (*aṣṭagraha sammelana*) on 10 March 1982, there would be a catastrophe and disastrous effects on the Earth. This was well publicized nationally by Indian astrologers and even internationally by Western astrologers. But that day was as uneventful as any other day. It was shown in advance by the astronomers that this configuration could have no perceptible effect on the Earth as the tidal force exerted by the other planets on the Earth was only 1/25,000th part of the force exerted together by the Moon and the Sun.

Remarkable vagueness of political forecasts made by late B.V. Raman, the doyen among the Indian astrologers, can also be cited. We all know that the January 1980 Lok Sabha elections brought Mrs Indira Gandhi back to power. This completely belied the confident predictions of almost all top Indian astrologers including B.V. Raman. In the *Astrological Magazine* (July 1979), the astrological prediction made by Raman was: "There is no indication of the Government or the Janata Party collapsing. Jupiter in the ascendant saves the situation." The sceptics of astrology are indeed grateful to Raman for obliging them by departing from his characteristic evasive vagueness in predictions. Moreover, no astrologer can lay claim on having predicted the most dramatic and momentous decision of Mrs Gandhi to declare national Emergency in 1975; nor did any astrologer predict the assassination of Mrs Gandhi in 1984.

Astrological features concerning weekly planetary influences on human life are regularly published in most of the newspapers of repute. Even astrologers admit that these features in newspaper columns have little reliable basis for prediction of the day's or week's events. Why then do so when many people believe that astrology works?

We have also the problem that the most popular house systems used by astrologers do not work in certain circumstances. As the astrophysicist Jean-Claude Pecker, writing in the interdisciplinary journal *Leonardo*, points out that a large number of human beings live in the southern and the northern polar regions of the Earth, where it is impossible to see any planet at any time during several months of the year. For example, the inhabitants of the large town of Murmansk in the Soviet Union spend about six months of the year without seeing the Sun, without seeing a sign of the zodiac and without seeing a planet. The people who are born in Murmansk during these "unfortunate" months, therefore, have no horoscope at all in an astrological sense. Nevertheless, they may become good scientists, excellent doctors, competent carpenters and even horrid criminals.

Then there is the time-twin problem – that is, the dissimilarity of individuals born at the same time. Many people also ask why astrologers assign significance to the time of birth rather than to the time of conception. If the planets affect me all my life, why did they not affect me before birth? If the force, whatever it is, can make itself felt over millions of kilometres of interplanetary space, are we to believe that it can be stopped by two inches of abdominal wall? As long as the astrologers continue to ask for the moment of birth instead of the moment of conception, they reveal that they have not thought about the consequences of their position. And even the moment of birth is suspect. When does it occur? When the head appears, or the whole body? And how does one determine the moment of birth in a Caesarian section? What is the moment of birth of a frog who was incubated in a test tube? And furthermore, what happens if my mother falls down the stairs in the last week of pregnancy, and I am born several days earlier than I am supposed to be? How do the planets adapt to this? Or was my mother's fall preordained or row managed somehow, in order that I might be born at the right moment?

Conclusion

In our country the uneducated and the half-educated account for nearly 95 per cent of the population. Quite obviously, a scientific mentality has eluded them. They fall prey to superstitions at every step, but do not feel the urge to prove the existence of sound logic behind these. However, those who consider themselves modern and highly educated also do have belief in various superstitions. Many a time I have seen university professors and highly literate scientists professing tremendous faith in astrology – a faith that is proudly displayed by three or four gemned rings on their fingers. How strange and sad! Those who themselves teach science compromise with pseudo-science and evil science. You teach science and strongly believe in astrology – this is nothing but living on falsehood. There is no doubt that such perverted behaviour on the part of our educated people is a grave obstacle to the development of our society. From what we have discussed so far, it clearly emerges that astrology is incapable of any change or rectification.

4

Scientific Outlook in Ancient Indian Academic Tradition

Ramkrishna Bhattacharya

THE topic I have been asked to speak on is so vast that it is impossible to do justice to even one of the aspects that constitute the "Ancient Indian Academic Tradition". It is not just a question of time allotted to the speaker in a seminar; every discipline cultivated in India except ritual literature and theology will have to be taken into account to evaluate the topic. Therefore, I have decided to confine myself to the following areas: (a) What is meant by "scientific outlook"? (b) How was it developed in ancient India? (c) How was its application to therapeutics and surgery thwarted by forces opposed to science?

Referring to an aphorism in the base text of the Cārvāka/ Lokāyata, Bimal Krishna Matilal observed: "This empirical methodology might have been the precursor of scientific thought in India" (1987: 165). The aphorism reads: "As the power of intoxication (arises or is manifested) from the constituent parts of the intoxicating drink (*kiṇva*, such as flour, water and molasses)".

Scientific outlook demands conviction in the materiality of the world and a method of ascertaining truth preferably by sense-perception, and if that is not possible, with the help of comparison (inference by analogy), but never is the "evidence" of word (*śabda*, verbal testimony) derived from religious texts, such as the Veda. Hence the motto of the Royal Society (the UK): "We take nobody's word for it" (*Nullius in verba*).

Scientific outlook implies rejection of all *āptavākyas*, even if they come from established scientists. The other maxim, "Let the experiment be made on a worthless body" (*fiat experimentum in corpore vili*) is also relevant in relation to the art and science of surgery in particular. One of the basic instructions in the *Suśruta Saṁhitā* is:

> Different parts of the body cannot be correctly described who is not versed in anatomy. Anyone who desires to acquire proper knowledge (*niḥsaṁśaya jñāna*) should prepare and carefully observe by dissecting it, and examine its different parts. A thorough knowledge can only be acquired by comparing the accounts seen in the Śāstras (text of anatomy) with direct observation. —Bhisagratna edn 3.5.49

Detailed instructions are provided as to how the body is to be studied.

Now the attitude of the authors of the Dharmaśāstras to the corpse was exactly the opposite (the examples that follow are taken from Chattopadhyaya 1982: 85). Āpastamba decrees:

> One must not study scripture in a village in which there is a corpse or in such a one where the *cāṇḍāla*s reside. One must not study where corpses are being carried to the boundary of a village. – 1.3.9.14-16

Gautama, another religious law-maker, provides a list of impure persons:

> On touching a *cāṇḍāla*, a woman impure on account of her confinement, a woman in her courses, a corpse, and on touching persons who have touched them, the person must purify himself. . . . – 14.30-32

And Manu states:

> When a man has touched a *cāṇḍāla*, a menstruating woman, an outcaste woman in child bed, a corpse, or one who has touched a corpse has to purify himself by bathing. – 5.85

This being the attitude towards "purity", it is too much to expect that the profession of a surgeon would be treated with honour.

It is not necessary to refer to the legends found in the *Yajurveda*, particularly the *Taittirīya Saṁhitā* (*TS*). There are stories about the

Aśvin brothers vis-à-vis the gods who ostracized them, for they were impure and moving among humans as physicians (*apūtau vā imau manuṣyacarau bhiṣajau iti*). The text finally declares:

> Since the physician is impure and unfit for sacrifice, a brāhmaṇa should not practise medicine (*tasmāt brāhmaṇena bheṣajaṁ na kāryam, apūtā hi eṣaḥ amedhyaḥ yaḥ bhiṣak) – Taittirīya Saṁhitā* 6.4.9

There are similar stories in other recensions of the *Taittirīya Saṁhita*, the *Vājasaneyī Saṁhitā* (the White *Yajurveda*), the *Śatapatha Brāhmaṇa* and in the *Mahābhārata*. (For a fuller treatment, see Chattopadhyaya 2014: 211-31.)

We have already seen how important was the study of anatomy from human corpses. Prafulla Chandra Ray, the first historian of Chemistry in India (which he called, following the then custom, "Hindu Chemistry") observed:

> According to Suśruta, the dissection of dead bodies is a *sine qua non* to the student of surgery and this high authority lays particular stress on knowledge gained from experiment and observation [Ray quotes from the *Suśruta Saṁhitā*, Śārīrasthāna, 5.43-45, 48]. But Manu would have none of it. The very touch of a corpse, according to Manu, is enough to bring contamination to the sacred person of [a] Brāhmin [Ray refers to the *Laws of Manu*, 5.64, 85, 87]. – Ray 1903: 192-93.

What was the outcome of Manu's fiat? Ray writes:

> Thus we find that shortly after the time of Vāgbhaṭa, the handling of a lancet was discouraged and Anatomy and Surgery fell into disuse and became to all intents and purposes lost sciences to the Hindus. –Ibid.

Not only surgery, but also therapeutics suffered from a strange anomaly. The two great medical compilations, the *Caraka Saṁhitā* and the *Suśruta Saṁhitā*, having been redacted and revised over many generations, have come down to us in a strange shape: both science and its opposite appear to coexist. The *Caraka Saṁhitā* (*CS*) is full of praise for gods, cows, brāhmaṇas, preceptors, elders, adepts and teachers (1.8.18 and passim). People are warned not to speak against the brāhmaṇas, nor to raise a stick against the cow (*na brāhmaṇān parivadet, na gavāṁ daṇḍa udyacchet*) (1.18.25). The premonitory symptoms of a particular form of exogenous insanity is said to be caused by the anger of the gods and others (2.7.11). What are the symptoms? They are the proclivity to hurt the gods, cows, brāhmaṇas and ascetics (2.7.11). There are so many other examples proclaiming the holiness of the cow in the *Caraka Saṁhitā* (see Chattopadhyaya 1982: 210-11).

Nevertheless, beef is found to be recommended as the diet of the patients suffering from "the loss of flesh due to disorder caused by an excess of *vāyu*, rhinitis, irregular fever, dry cough, fatigue, and cases of excessive appetite due to hard manual labour" (1.27.79-80).

This is only one of the many instances in which the flesh of cows, and of buffaloes, horses, goats, and even of elephants, are prescribed (see *CS* 6.1.183). It is curious to observe that the learned authors of *A Review of "Beef in Ancient India"* (Gita Press, Gorakhpur, 1971, enlarged second edition Shree Krishna Janmasthan Seva-Sansthan, Mathura, 1983) have taken no notice of the prescription of beef for patients in the *Caraka Saṁhitā*. The book is purported to be a refutation of Rajendra Lal Mitra's essay mentioned in the title. The omission of beef in dietetics cannot but be deliberate.

How could the recommendation of beef in the dietetics and the veneration of the cow on a par with the gods, brāhmaṇas and others be reconciled? One may speak of the special capacity inherent in the culture and civilization of India for admitting all discord and turn them into concord. Such a mystical quality, however, is not found when the powers that be dealt with what they consider to be heretical, heterodox, or downright non-Vedic. So long as there is relative peace and prosperity, opposition to the mainstream ideas is, or rather, can be, tolerated, at least up to a certain extent. The extent will be decided by considering the threat such opposition poses to the *varṇa* and *āśrama* system, the model of social system in India formulated in the *Kauṭilīya Arthaśāstra* (fourth century BCE). But when the ideas are irreconcilable, such as protection of the cow and the recommendation of her flesh in the diet of a patient, the situation becomes precarious. The doctors could save their science only by paying lip service to orthodoxy, as did the astronomers. They too had to submit to the Vedic view regarding the causes of the solar and lunar eclipses. Brahmagupta and Varāhamihira are cases in point. The worst was the fate of Āryabhaṭa. He had proposed a geokinetic hypothesis, as against the current geostatic view. Later writers on astronomy not only misinterpreted him; they also tampered the text of the *Āryabhaṭīyam*, thereby making him say what he had never said (for a fuller discussion, see R. Bhattacharya 1990-91: 35-47).

Acknowledgements

Thanks are due to Amitava Bhatacaryya, Gopa Basu. Siddhartha Dutta and Sunish Kumar Deb. for their support. The usual disclaimers apply.

Works Cited

Bhattacharya, Ramkrishna, 1990-91, "The Case of Āryabhaṭa and His Detractors", *The Indian Historical Review*, 17(1-2): 35-47.

Bhishagratna, Kunjalal (tr.), 1981, *The Suśruta Saṁhitā*, vol. II, Varanasi: Chowkhambha Sanskrit Series Office (first published in 1911).

Charakasaṁhitā, The, ed. P.M. Mehta et al., Jamnagar: Gulabkunverba Ayurvedic Society, 1949.

Chattopadhyaya, Debiprasad, 1982, "Case for a Critical Analysis of the Caraka-Saṁhitā", in *Studies in the History of the Science in India*, vol. 1, ed. Debiprasad Chattopadhyaya, New Delhi: Editorial Enterprises.

Chattopadhyaya, 2014, "*Science and Society in Ancient India*, Kolkata: K.P. Bagchi (first published, 1977).

Matilal, B.K., 1987, "Cārvāka", in *Encyclopedia of Religion*, vol. 3 New York: Macmillan.

Ray, P.C., 1903, *History of Hindu Chemistry*, vol. 1, 2nd edn, Calcutta: The Bengal Chemical and Pharmaceutical Works.

Suśruta Saṁhitā, ed. Ambikādatta Śāstri, Varanasi: Chaukhambha Sanskrit Sansthan, 1987 (first published in 1953).

5

Ancient Indian Cosmology vis-à-vis Modern Scientific Cosmology

Dhirendranath Banerjee

In comparison to the vast and endless universe (presently called multiverse) our mother earth is simply one of the tiniest particles of the whole creation. It is still a mystery how and when and why did it come into existence. Long long ago intelligent man (*homo sapiens*) started questioning about the origin of creation including the earth, the sky, the sun, the stars and as a whole about the universe around him. This concept is now known as cosmogony, cosmology or creation science. But human interest on this subject is as old as human civilization and has been discussed in all ancient writings of the world. How did this world come into existence? This was one of the fundamental questions of human mind and discussed throughout 4000–5000 years. In Sanskrit language it is known as *sarga* or creation (*sṛṣṭi-tattva*, i.e. the theory of creation of the world). In English it is cosmology, i.e. *kosmos*, world, *logos* study (study on the origin of the universe). Many scholars value cosmology as a "historical science" or the "most ancient science of the human race". Metaphysical cosmology has put man and his identity in relation to all other entities of the universe around him. Physical cosmology deals with the structure of the universe, constituents of the universe – planets, stars, galaxies along with elementary particles like dark matter and dark energy. Cosmology is the science of origin and evolution of the physical world. Present-day scholars have classified the different theories of cosmology into various classes. Cosmology is chiefly concerned with the world as totally the whole of space, time and every phenomenon. The two principal divisions of cosmology are metaphysical cosmology and scientific cosmology. The first one is chiefly concerned with philosophical method and differs from religious cosmology which is mainly God-oriented though sometimes a few atheistic religious-philosophical schools are purely materialistic in their approach. At present metaphysical cosmology is chiefly concerned with the following:

(a) How did the universe come into being?
(b) What is the ultimate material component of the universe?
(c) Does the universe have a purpose?
(d) What is the first cause in the origin of the universe?
(e) Is it possible to know the whole mystery of the universe?
(f) Is there any conscious being behind the creation?
(g) Can we explain metaphysical truth through cosmological reasoning?

In the Upaniṣads we come across such questions: Is *Brahman* the first cause? Where do we come from? By whom we have been living in this world? How do we live between good and evil, pain and pleasure?

The titles of two Upaniṣads are interesting – *Kena* (meaning "by whom") and *Praśna* (meaning inquiry/controversy/debate). The *Annapūrṇā Upaniṣad* begins with some fundamental questions of philosophy – Who am I? Why does this world come into existence? What is the nature of cosmology? Why do life and death both exist?

In the Upaniṣads different views about the creation of the world have been given and these are as follows:

- Prajāpati (the Creator) desired progeny. He practised *tapas* He created male and female (*mithuna*) (*Praśnopaniṣad* 1.4).
- In the begining it was *asat* (void). Then *sat* (matter) came out of *asat*. From this all things were created (*Taittirīya Upaniṣad* 7.1).
- In the beginning it was *ātman* or Supreme One, Self-existent Consciousness and the Uncaused Cause. There was no other thing except that (*Aitareya Upaniṣad* 1.1.1).
- But how is it that *sat* came into existence from *asat*? It was, therefore, *sat* in the beginning (*Chāndogy'opaniṣad* 6.2.2)

- It was neither *sat* nor *asat*, but *sad–asat*. The gradual development is as follows: *sat–asat* → darkness (void) → elemental universe sky → wind → heat → water → earth (in the form of an egg, i.e. *brahmāṇḍa / hiraṇyāṇḍa* → divided into two parts – earth and the sky.

Ultimately *Paramātman / Brahman* (the Supreme Soul) has been proclaimed as the *summum bonum* of this material world and the ultimate goal of our life is to know him and thus emancipation comes through union with *Brahman*.

In Biblical Genesis, God created the universe out of nothing (*creatio ex nihilo*). In ancient Indian six traditional philosophical schools and other athesitic schools like Jaina and Buddhist schools different theories of cosmology are to be found. Vedānta school proclaims purely divine cosmology, while Nyāya–Vaiśeṣika gives a theory of semi-divine cosmology. According to Nyāya, atoms of four elements are eternal like God Himself, and due to God's desire there starts a reaction among the atoms, and finally the material world comes into being. The Sāṁkhya, Jaina and Buddhist proclaim materialistic theory of cosmology. In the *Śvetāśvatara Upaniṣad* we come across the materialistic theories prevalent during that period. In this Upaniṣad the number of questions put before the preceptor is as follows: "Is *Brahman* the cause of creation?", "Whence do we come from?" and "How do we live?"

To this question the teacher refers to the following theories: *kāla* (time), *svabhāva* (nature of things), *niyati* (destiny), *yadṛcchā* (chance) and *bhūta* (four elements). According to Nyāya–Vaiśeṣika, time and space (*kāla* and *dik*) are eternal, but Vedānta does not accept this theory. These are the anti-theories of Divine Creationism. The *Śvetāśvatara Upaniṣad* just refers to these theories casually and does not explain such terms. In the second verse of 6th chapter *svabhāva* and *kāla* (nature and time) theories out of these five have been referred to and also criticized the folly of their followers. The Vedānta does not accept time or atom as eternal. Some Western philosophers (both ancient and modern like Xeno, Plato, Spinoza and Hegel) did not accept time as eternal.

According to Aristotle, the ever-changing nature of things

is the real concept of time. Time is both linear and circular. The concept of time in modern scientific concept and the ancient theory is quite different and it is the simple equation $T = O$. According to the Big Bang (or expanding theory of universe) theory, the concept of time and space is relative.

According to the *svabhāva* theory, the nature of things has been the cause of this creation. *Niyati* means fixed order of things, i.e. necessity or destiny or fate. *Yadṛcchā* (chance/accident/chaos/randomness) means that this universe is an accidental creation out of void and there is not any kind of *Intelligent Design*. For some, *asat* means "primeval state before creation, undivided mass with all discontent" or "elements congested in shapeless heap". Ancient Greek philosopher Leucippus believed in atomic theory. But he admits some kind of chance or accident in the reaction of atoms. Thus he says:

> The cosmos then became like a spherical form in this way: the atoms being submitted to a casual unpredictable movement quickly and instantly. The matter by virtue of its own active force, moves and acts in a blind way.

Therefore, according to him, this cosmos is really an accidental creation and it is absolutely useless to seek any logic or reason behind it. Darwin in his famous work *Origin of Species through Natural Selection* also gives importance to chance in the origin of life in this world. *Niyati* is fixed order of things, destiny or fate. Destiny and fatalism are sometimes the same. In the Vanaparva of the *Mahābhārata* Yudhiṣṭhira explains the theories of Svabhāvavāda, Daivavāda and Karmavada (Inherent Nature of Matter, Destiny and Action). Due to their pitiable condition Draupadī casts aspertion on God for his indifference towards the good people and brings the common complaint against the so-called omnibenevolent God – God does not care for the good but, on the contrary, favours the corrupt. Then Draupadī refers to the popular atheistic views: "Some say that in this world everything happens because of its own nature." "Others say that it is destiny or fatalism." To this, Yudhiṣṭhira replies: Oh Draupadī, you are speaking like an atheist (*nāstikyaṁ tu prabhāṣase*). The sceptics decry

God due to their stupidity. They do not accept other arguments and discard them."

Again in the Anuśāsana-Parva Bhīṣma, while advising Yudhiṣṭhira on different topics of ethics and morality, refers to *daiva, puruṣakāra, svabhāva, kāla,* etc. and remarks in this context that all such theories are false and only the heretics do not believe in God and do not accept the arguments of the theists. According to Jaina and Buddhist schools, creation starts with matter. This may be called atomism or quantum cosmology at present (atom/proton/electron/positron/quark).

Theory of material cosmology has been classified as:

(i) Scientific materialism,

(ii) dialectical materialism,

(iii) physiological materialism, and

(iv) vulgar or popular materialism.

From ancient to the modern times we come across different theories regarding the origin of the universe. In religious and other classes of wisdom literature, this branch of knowledge is known as cosmogony or cosmology or creation science. This is one of the fundamental questions of human mind – how did this world or universe (at present multiverse) come into existence? Almost all scriptures and religious codes and works on astronomy and other branches of ancient science deal with this question in their own way and there is close similarity in the scrutiny of human thought-process. Ancient Indian literature – the Vedas, Purāṇas, the *Mahābhārata* and Smr̥tis – had raised this question. Among the five principal features of Purāṇic literature the following three are concerned with cosmology – *sarga, pratisarga* and *manvantara* (i.e. creation, temporary annihilation and start of new creation after the end of one phase of creation in a certain period of 15,70,00,000 years). Creation and destruction (*sr̥ṣṭi* and *pralaya*) are the two features of this phenomenal world and there is no end to this existence and thus it is *ad infinitum.*

Different theories of cosmology may be classified under the following heads:

1. Divine creationism
2. Semi-divine creationism
3. Material creationism
4. Quantum creationism.

In other way, we may classify the theories thus:

1. Sceptic/agnostic theory
2. Theistic/atheistic theory
3. Materialistic theory.

Some modern scientists have given another class of division:

1. Religious-cum-mytho-physical cosmology
2. Dialectical cosmology
3. Philosophical cosmology
4. Historical cosmology.

Almost all religions of the world share the view that God, the Eternal, Supreme Infinite, the Omniscient, is the creator of this world. Out of his own will he created everything through his divine power. In ancient Indian tradition the concept of cosmology has many different theories starting from divine to material creationism. The six schools of traditional Indian philosophy propounded their own views which are not similar and also contradictory. The Vedānta, Nyāya–Vaiśeṣika, Sāṁkhya and Mīmāṁsā schools have their own separate theories. The Vedānta accepts boldly the theory of divine creationism. The Nyāya theory may be called semi-divine in nature. But the Sāṁkhya theory does not accept God or any such Supreme Being as the authority of the universe. The theory of divine creation is very simple and based on belief in the Almighty; thus it says that God created everything according to his own power and will with the elements of his own.The Biblical theory in Genesis is also formulated in very simple way – God created this phenomenal world along with all sorts of creatures and last of all human beings in his own image (*creatio ex nihilo*, i.e. creation out of nothing). In Nyāya–Vaiśeṣika it is claimed that atoms of four elements are eternal like God and even after *pralaya* (annihilation of the world) atoms remain dormant since these are the indivisible particles of the elemental world and again form into matter by the willpower of God. The various theories of cosmology in given in Table 5.1.

Table 5.1: Classification of the Theories of Cosmology

Classification	*Author/Literature Date*	*Classification*	*Feature*
Vedic/Upaniṣadic	3000–800 BCE	Cyclical/ oscillating	Divine action
Jaina Cosmology	Jaina Āgamas Teachings of Mahāvīra (599-527 BCE)	*Loka* (universe) is self-created	Automatic Infinite, no beginning or end
Buddhist Cosmology	Teachings of Buddha, Bauddha/ Āgama literature	Self-existent	ad infinitum Material creation
Babylonian Cosmology	Babylonian Literature (3000 BCE)	Flat earth from water creation	Infinite waters earth and hevean state of choas
Eleatic Cosmology	Parmenides	Finite and spherical	Infinite, uniform perfect, not void
Biblical Cosmology	Genesis (*c*.10000 BCE)	Earth floaing	Earth and heaven form a unit, while firmament forms a separate unit
Atomic Universe	Anaxagoras (500–428 BCE) Hindu (600– CE)	Infinite	Earth made of indivisible atoms. All objects decay, but new creation starts, Everlasting atom
Atomic	Creation	Cause and effect	Through some unknown cause, not chaos
Pythagorean theory	Pythogoras (570–495 BCE)	Central fire burning for	The sun, the moon and other planets ever revolving round the central fire
De Mundo	(350–200 BCE)	Two regions: a variety of Aristotelian theory	Total five regions constituted of five elements: earth, water, air, fire and ether

Cont.

Table 5.1: ***Cont.***

Classification	*Author/Literature Date*	*Classification*	*Feature*
Stoic Theory	Ancient Greak scholars	The great island	Cosmos surrounded by infinite void, world in a state of flux, pulsating and undergoing changes
Aristotelian Cosmology	(384-322 BCE)	Geocentric, steady state, finite extent	Earth is spherical, universe eternal and changeless, four known elements plus ether
Aristarchean Model	Aristarchus (*c*.280 BCE)	Heliocentric	Earth rotates on its own axis and moves round the sun in a circular way. The stars and planets are fixed centring the sun
Ptolemaic Model	Ptolemy (100-170 CE)		Earth remains in centre. Stars and planets are moving round the earth in circular epicycles
Āryabhaṭa Model	Āryabhaṭa (476–550 CE)	Geocentric	Earth rotates on its own axis. Planets move in elliptical orbits round the earth or sun
Medieval Period	Philosophical: Christian/ Islamic		Ancient theory of philosophers discarded, Biblical genesis supported finite and fixed earth

Classification	*Author/Literature Date*	*Classification*	*Feature*
Nīlakaṇṭha Model	Nīlakaṇṭha Somayaji (1444–1544)	Geocentric/ heliocentric	Planets rotate round the sun. Sun moves round the earth
Copernican Model	Copernicus (1473–1543)	Heliocentric universe	Planets move round the sun
Tycho Brahe	Tycho Brahe (1546–1601)	Geocentric/ heliocentric	Planets orbit the sun, the sun orbits the earth
Bruno Model	Giordano Bruno (1548–1600)	Infinite space and time	All objects made of void filled with ether, the planets and earth consist of same property
Kepler Model	Johannes Kepler (1571–1630)	Heliocentric	Based on mathematical physical theory, elliptical planetary orbit
Newton Model	Isaac Newton (1643–1727)	Static and evolving	Infinite universe, all particles mutually attracting, matter uniformly distributed
Einstein Model	Albert Einstein (1879–1955)	Static and finite	Space curved and spherical, expanding universe
De Sitter Model	William de Sitter (1872–1934)	Steady state	Expanding space, based on Einstein's general theory of relativity
Big Bang Theory	Alexander Friedmann (1888–1925), Georges Lemaitre (1894–1966)	Expanding universe	A super-dense atom got burst and followed by a two-stage expansion.

Divine cosmology is very simple in theory. With firm belief it proclaims:

> The unchanging, infinite, immanent and transcendent reality which is the divine ground of all matter, energy, time, space, being and everything beyond this universe, that is the one supreme, universal spirit, – the highest universal spirit, – the highest universal principle, – the ultimate reality in the universe, the material-efficient-formal and final cause of all that exists.
> – According to Paul Deussen in the English translation of Upaniṣad

The theory of creation as propounded in Genesis of the Old Testament has been discarded by some modern scientists as simply "Biblical nonsense". But in the same vein we cannot declare Upaniṣadic creationism as absurd, because there is some sort of scientific outlook in some of their hypotheses. For example at least one view may be quoted: God → sky → wind → heat → water → earth (gradual development of cosmos). God's divine creation and intelligent design is ignored by modern scientists as "omnipotent paradox". Although there is some sort of unitary thinking and logical approach among the Upaniṣadic views some mythical and folk elements are also amalgamated. Following the Vedic tradition the *Mahābhārata*, the Purāṇas, Smṛtis, astronomical works and other sorts of various texts have discussed the theories of creation and mainly the Vedic–Upaniṣadic theories as well as the theories of six philosophical schools have been taken into consideration. Out of five principal features of Purāṇa the first two (i.e. *sarga* and *pratisarga* or primary creation and secondary creation) are directly connected with cosmology. It is interesting to note that all the Purāṇas (Mahā Purāṇas and Upa Purāṇas) have accepted the Sāṁkhya theory of creation (i.e. in brief creation started through the combination of matter and spirit). In the Nāsadīya Sūkta of the *Ṛgveda* (X.2.129), the Vedic seer expresses sceptic views about the origin of the world:

> There was neither *asat* nor *sat* in the beginning; there was no particle, nor the endless sky; neither death nor non-death; there was darkness enveloped in deep darkness; everything was immersed in abyss of water.

Then he asks:

> "Who really knows it"? (i.e. how the creation started)? How did this material world come into being? Even the gods are later creations. Then who knows whence does this material world come first? He who is the Supreme Lord in the eternal space may or may not know this.

In this hymn two main questions of cosmology are asked:"Whence" and "how" did the universe come into being?

If we consider the Vedas as a whole, divine cosmology is the foundation of Vedic philosophy. In the Upaniṣads different theories have been propounded and they bear some unity among them. The views of the Upaniṣadic scholars are as follows:

> Prajāpati (the Creator) desired progeny; he practised penance and created male and female. – *Praśnopaniṣad* 1.4

> Otherwise in the beginning it was *asat* or void, thereafter *sat* came into force, i.e. creation started. Creation began when *Ātman* himself pressed himself into the work of creation.
> – *Taittirīya Upaniṣad* 7.1

> In the beginning it was *Ātman*, the One and only One. Besides him nothing remained. Then he desired – let me create the worlds. – *Aitareya Upaniṣad* 1.1.1

> In the beginning it was only *sat*, the One singular state. But others say that in the beginning it was *asat*, the One and only One. From this *asat*, *sat* came into existence. – *Chāndogyopaniṣad* 6.2.1

In all these views there are three fundamental principles – *sat*, *asat* and creator God. So the Upaniṣadic cosmology is fundamentally divine cosmology, a mixture of theological and metaphysical concepts. There are many other views based on divine creationism. But some scholars think that the real cause of the origin of creation of this universe is shrouded in mystery and even today, in an advanced stage of astrophysics and astronomy, some scholars claim that the state before the Big Bang or the cause of Big Bang cannot be scientifically ascertained.

One fundamental question of creation in science is: is this world eternal, i.e. without beginning or end? Or is this creation temporary, i.e. it has beginning as well as end? In different traditions of religious–philosophical creationism, end of creation or annihilation has been explained through different time factors. In Indian Vedic–Purāṇic–astronomical concept, end of creation has been conceived as temporary and eternal (*khaṇḍapralaya* and *mahāpralaya*). Different theories of temporary or permanent annihilation are as follows:

Indian: In one *kalpa* (eon), i.e. 10 × 8.64 years complete one cycle.

(According to the *Sūrya Siddhānta,* Kali era started in 3102 BCE. After 420,000 years total annihilation will be completed.)

Babylonian: one cycle = 12,690,000 years.

Greek: eternal creation (neither beginning nor end).

Roman: one cycle = 1,000 years.

Chinese: one cycle = 23,639,000 years.

Christian: one cycle = 6,000–7,000 years.

Some special features of ancient Indian astronomical cosmology are as follows:

Īśvara → Hiraṇyagarbha/Prajāpati/Brahmā → viśva
(Supreme God→ Creator God → universe).

The theory of geocentric universe was almost common to all ancient civilizations of the world (India, Greece, Mesopotamia, China) and this theory was prevalent up to the Middle Ages.

In India Āryabhaṭa (fifth century CE) established the theory of motion of earth (i.e. Bhū-Bhramaṇa-Vāda or the theory of moving earth; but it was not accepted by later scholars of astronomy barring a few.

The position of earth and other planets like sun, moon, etc. was calculated by Indian astronomers:

Earth → Sun → Moon → Stars → Venus → Jupiter → Saturn
→ Saptarṣi pole star.

Their mutual difference between each other is 100,000 *yojanas*

(1 *yojana*= 2.5/4/5/9 miles).

On the basis of distance the position of planets from the earth is estimated thus:

Moon → Mercury → Venus → Sun → Mars → Jupiter → Saturn.

In modern astrological calculation planets in relation to the sun are situated thus:

Sun → Mercury → Venus → Earth → Mars → Jupiter → Saturn → Uranus → Neptune → Pluto.

Different theories of creation science are given in brief with model graphs.

Pythagoras' Theory of Cosmology

Pythagoras (578–495 BCE) believed that the sun, moon, earth and other planets have been moving around a great central fire. All these are enclosed in a hollow sphere or vast globe where innumerable stars are hanging.

Geocentric Theory of Aristotle (384-322 BCE) and Claudius Ptolemqeus (150 CE)

Earth lies in the centre of the universe. The sun, moon and other planets are moving around earth in circular orbits. Ptolemy believed that each planet moves in a small circle or epicycle, the centre of which, the deterent itself, moved round the earth in a perfect circle.

Aristarchus (310–230 BCE) proposed heliocentric theory for the first time. But it did not get much support due to the popular geocentric theory formulated by Plato and Aristotle as well as Roman Church.

Nicholaus Copernicus (1473–1543) assumed that the sun is in the centre. Due to this new idea many problems of the theory of Ptolemy were removed. But Copernicus supported the idea of circular orbits.

Tycho Brahe (1546–1601) proposed a new theory in which he tried to establish that the earth lies in the centre of the universe and the planets are moving around the sun in a circular way. He collected many valuable information about cosmology when telescope was not invented.

Johanese Kepler (1571–1630) interpreted Brahe's data and developed a few empirical laws by which the behaviour of the planets could be ascertained.

Galileo Galilee (1564–1642) for the first time used telescope and studied the sky for several years and made important and critical observations by which heliocentric theory was unanimously accepted.

Isaac Newton (1643–1727) discovered some physical laws which explained the reason behind the moving of the planets around the sun.

Heliocentric Universe: Here we see eleven planets placed in their position in relation to the sun in distance – Mercury, Venus, Earth, Mars, Jupiter, Saturn, Uranus, Neptune, Pluto, Makemake and Eris. Broken parts of some ancient planet burst due to strong gravitational force believed to be scattered on the vast space between Mars and Jupiter.

Solar system: Planets moving round the sun elliptically.

The sun: The sun is the nearest star visible from our planet earth during day time. Its distance from earth is 149,597,870.7 km. Diameter= 13,93,000 km. Temperature = 15×10^6 °c (on the core), 600 °C on the surface). It is 109 times greater than our earth. Constituents = 90 per cent hydrogen and 24.8 per cent helium. Mass = 1.981×10^{30} kg (i.e. 2.91×10^{27} ton). Age = 5 billion years.

Our mother planet Earth is moving round the sun elliptically in a speed of 1,700 km per hour. The moon is the only a minor planet orbiting the earth.

Nine planets – Mercury, Venus, Earth, Mars, Jupiter, Saturn, Uranus, Neptune and Pluto – orbit the Sun elliptically.

Introduction to Different Models of the Universe/Multiverse

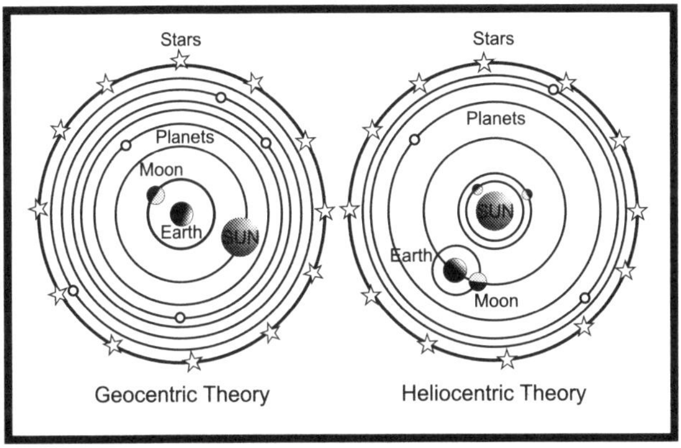

fig. 5.1: Geocentric and heliocentric theory

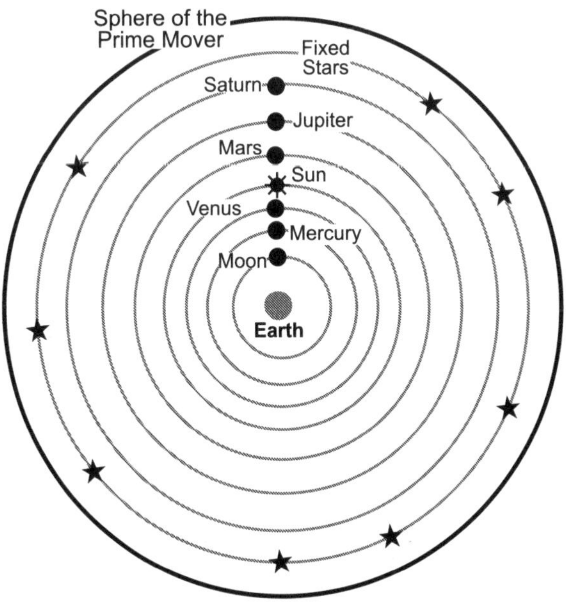

fig. 5.2: Aristotles's universe (geocentric model)

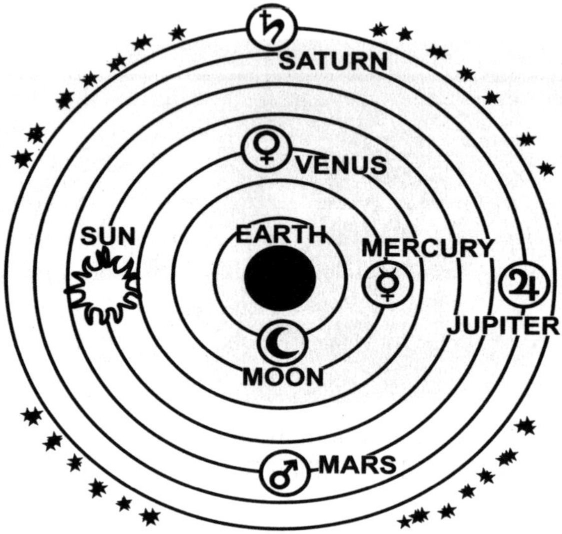

fig. 5.3: The most common theory prevalent in ancient China, Greece, India, Mesopotamia et al.

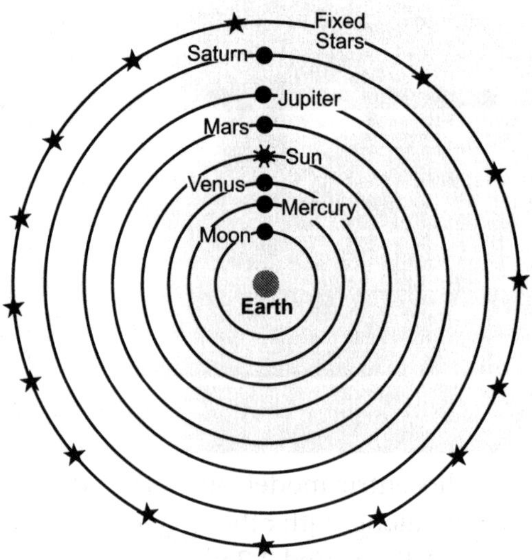

fig. 5.4: Ptolemaic model of geocentric theory

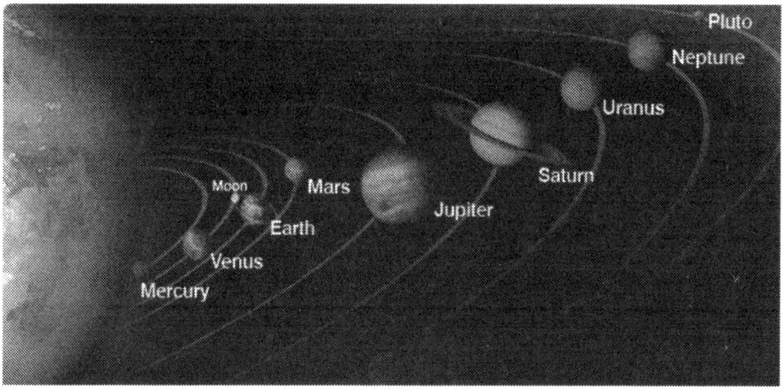

fig. 5.5: Solar system model of our universe introduced by Galileo Galilee (1643–1727)

fig. 5.6: Heliocentric model (sun – the nearest star from our Earth along with other planets, plus recently discovered 2-3 planets)

fig. 5.7: Geocentric/heliocentric model (Somayaji, Giordano Bruno, Isaac Newton, Albert Einstein)

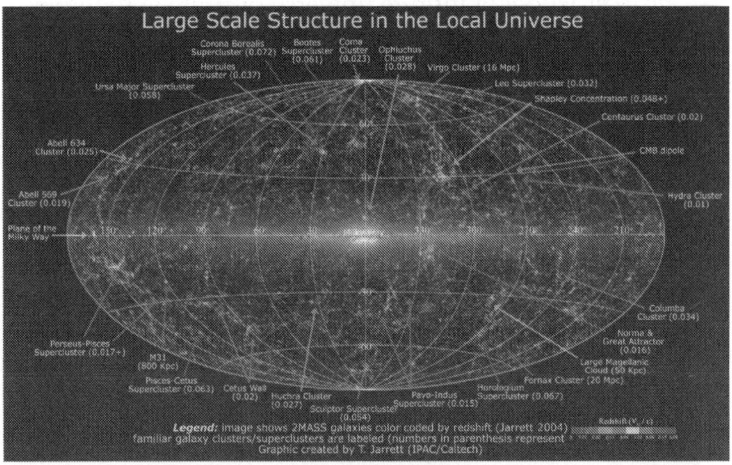

fig. 5.8: Local universe (elliptical planetary orbit based on mathematical/physical theory)

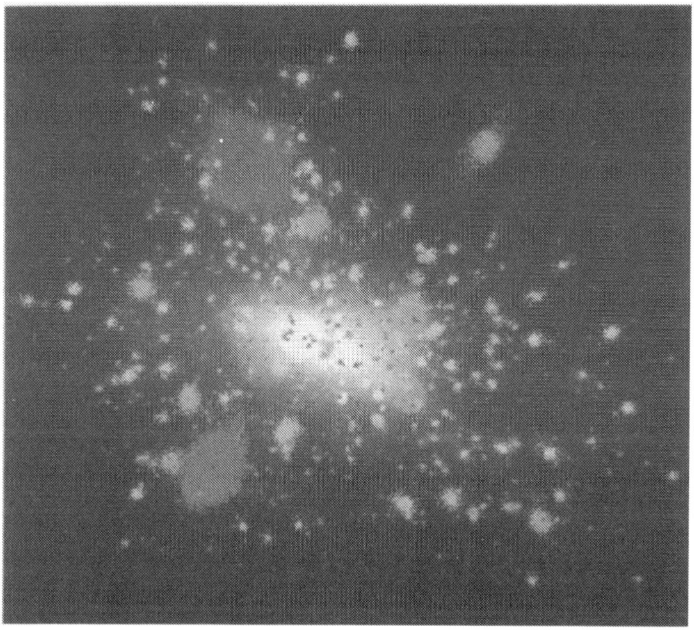

fig. 5.9: Model of infinite universe (infinite void/ether, particles mutually attracting)

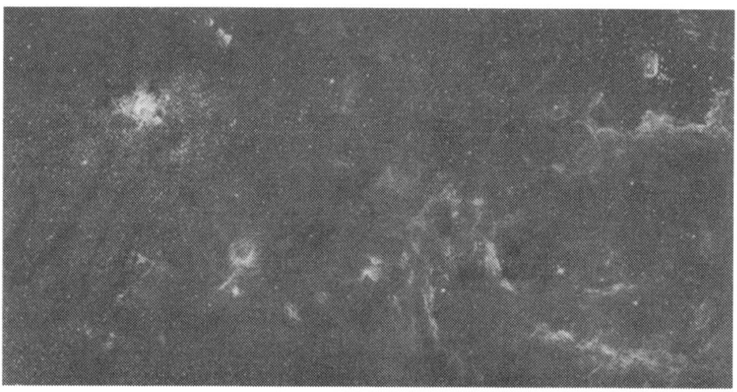

fig. 5.10: Expanding universe (De Setter, Albert Einstein, Alexander Friedmann and others): Big Bang/multiverse

6

The Concept of Matter
A Philosophy–Physics Interface

Raghunath Ghosh

THIS paper concentrates on the concept of matter in Indian tradition and its dynamic character. There is an eternal dispute between the spiritualists and materialists regarding the supremacy of matter and spirit. The spiritualists emphasize that spirit is real while matter is unreal. The materialists demand that matter is real and spirit is unreal. Sri Aurobindo is of the opinion that both are correct. In fact, what is called matter is nothing but non-manifested *sat*-element of the spirit called *Saccidānanda*.[1] Before this amalgamated theory, some of the Indian thinkers believed and propagated the dynamic character of matter which can create, destroy and sustain the whole universe. Among these thinkers Cārvākas are the forerunners who are of the opinion that matter (*bhūta*) is of four types – earth (*kṣiti*), water (*ap*), fire (*teju*) and air (*marut*) – which constitute human body. The consciousness has no separate existence apart from the amalgamation of the four just as red colour is manifested out of the amalgamation of lime, nut, etc.[2] That is why a dead body is dissolved in the elements. From this it is proved that elements or *bhūta*s have an in-built power to create something.

---

[1] *The Complete Works of Sri Aurobindo*, vol. 21: *The Life Divine*, pp. 8-29, Pondicherry: Sri Aurobindo Ashram, 2005.

[2] Sāyaṇa Mādhava, 1996, *Sarvadarśanasaṁgraha*, Cārvākadarśana, tr. Satyajyoti Chakraborty, Kolkata: Sahityashri, p. 1 (text portion only):

tatra pṛthivyādīni bhūtāni catvāri tattvāni ।
tebhya eva dehākārapariṇatebhyaḥ kiṇvādibhyo madaśaktivat caitanyamupajāyate ॥

In the Vaiśeṣika philosophy it has been accepted just like Quantum Physics that the world was originated as a result of combination of atoms, which is called Paramāṇukāraṇatāvāda as opposed to Brahmākaraṇatāvāda admitted by the Advaita Vedāntins. At the initial stage, two atoms were conjoined resulting in the formation of dyadic compound (*dvyaṇuka*). Three dyadic compounds gave rise to a triadic one called *trasareṇu* and in this way a gross object was originated. A question arises how two atoms that are matters or unconscious become conjoined without any conscious force.[3] To Sāṁkhya the atoms have got energy of their own leading to their combination. Conjunction in case of creation and disjunction in case of dissolution occur spontaneously due to having in-built power in an atom. Both are taken to be the sports of Nature possible through its auto-generated nature. Hence there is no need of admitting any other force or God-particle in the phenomenon of conjunction and disjunction of atoms.[4]

Hence no tension can be entertained among the physicists, specially in Quantum Physics, regarding the acceptance of some conscious principle. That a metallic object has got in-built power is evidenced from the following experiment. When a hot metal work from a blacksmith is found having yellow colour or orange colour, it is visible due to the visibility of the thermal radiation emitted by high temperature. Everything else is glowing with thermal radiation as well, but less brightly and at larger wavelengths than the human eye can detect. When it is cold, such object looks perfectly black, because it absorbs all the lights that fall on it and emits none. Consequently, an ideal thermal emitter is known as a black body and the radiation it emits is called black body *radiation*.[5]

---

3 *Vedāntadaśanam (Brahmasūtra with Śāṅkarabhāṣya)*, Tarkapāda adhyāya, tr. Swami Viśvarūpānanda Cipananda, vol. II, Kolkata: Udbodhan, 1996, pp. 272-300.

4 Ibid., pp. 215-40.

5 L. Mondel and E. Wolf, 1995, *Optical Coherence and Quantum Optics*, chap. 13, New York: Cambridge University Press; D. Kondepudi and I. Prigogine, 1998, *Modern Thermodynamics from Heat Engines to Dissipative Structures*, chap. 11, New York: John Wiley and Sons.

When three constituents of *Prakṛti* are in the state of equilibrium, there is creation. If this equilibrium is disturbed due to overpowering of one constituent, creation starts. Change is the mark of existence as envisaged by the Buddhists – *yat sat tat kṣaṇikam* and *arthakriyākāritvalakṣaṇam sat.*[6] If *pradhāna* is not transformed (*vikārī*), there is no change or creation. Change occurs automatically in *Prakṛti* due to its dynamic character (*svayambhū*). Creation needs activity and motion among the *guṇa*s. Without opposition, which is possible through disturbance in equilibrium, no creation is possible. That is why, thesis, anti-thesis and syntheses are taken as methods of creativity (cf. *sakal dvanda-birodha-majhe jagrata je bhalo*).

A.B.N. Seal has explained the three constituents – *sattva, raja*s and *tamas* – as essence, energy and mass. The first is the cause of self-illumination and others' illumination, second is the cause of action and the third is the cause of obstruction (*bādhakasvarūpa*). The illuminating character is transparent and useful in any disinterested pleasure. The third is a balancing factor capable of controlling others. These three cannot remain in a separate manner and hence they are called *guṇa*s (binding factors). In the case of immovable matter *tamas* is patent, *rajas* is latent and *sattva* is sublatent. In the case of movable matter *rajas* is patent, *tamas* is latent, *sattva* is sublatent. An object may seem to be the cause of happiness, misery and infatuation to someone due to having three elements in *Prakṛti.*[7] It is just like a girl who creates happiness to someone whom she loves, becomes the cause of misery to some whom she left and becomes indifferent to someone whom she does not know. Nature becomes balanced due to harmonization of three constituents of it just as our body becomes balanced due to having three constituents – wind (*vāyu*), bile (*pitta*) and cough (*kapha*) in a proportionate way. The Sāṁkhya philosophers have taken another metaphor to point out this truth. Just as a lamp keeps burning due to having mutual cooperation among three

[6] Sāyaṇa Mādhava, 1996, *Sarvadarśanasaṁgraha*, Bauddhadarśana, p. 6.

[7] Seal, Brajendranath, 2001, *The Positive Sciences of the Ancient Hindus*, Kolkata: Sahitya-Samsad, p. 2 (henceforth *Positive Sciences*).

factors – light (*agni*), wick (*vartti*) and oil (*taila*), *Prakṛti* can work with mutual cooperation of three constituents. A girl becomes such due to different situations and difference of person. It is the nature of sandal to provide happiness, but it may not seem to be so if other factors are not favourable to it. It may become the cause of unhappiness if it is applied in the winter. A camel can enjoy thrones and hence it is the cause of happiness to it. But to other animals thrones become the cause of unhappiness due to having different type of skin, etc. Natural qualities are not manifested due to having some impediment (*pratibandhakatā*).[8]

Among the three constituents (*guṇas*) *sattva* is the balancing factor. One who is overpowered with *sattva* quality is called *sāttvika*. According to the Sāṁkhya system, *rajoguṇa* makes an individual fickle-minded and lunatic while *tamoguṇa* makes one infatuated leading him to the world of inertia and frustration. Both *tamas* and *rajas* are the factors which make an individual imbalanced. That is why *sattva guṇa* alone makes a man tranquillized and calm. Under this stage a man can have artistic creativity, aesthetic enjoyment and exercise his creative (*kārayitrī*) and appreciative (*bhāvayitrī*) genius (*pratibhā*). The glory of such *sattva guṇa* is found in the emotional mood involved in grief which gives rise to the realization of joy. How is joy realized from the painful situations? In this situation our mind is absorbed in the performances and this absorption depends on the equilibrium of mind. When our mind is disturbed due to the non-equilibrium of three attributes of *sattva*, *rajas* and *tamas*, the pain follows. If our mind remains in the state of aesthetic experience, there is something which forcibly snatches our mind and keeps it in a state of complete rest (*viśrānti*) (*... rajastamovaicitryānuviddha-sattvamaya-nija-cit svabhāva-nivṛtirśrānti-lakṣaṇah ...*).[9] At this stage an individual's mind attains real rest, which is characterized by the taste of its own blissful consciousness dominated by the *sattva* quality along

[8] *Sāṁkhyakārikā* with *Tattvakaumudī*, *kārikā* 11, tr. Nararyan Chandra Goswami, pp. 146-50, Kolkata: Sanskrit Pustak Bhandar, 1982.

[9] *Dhvanyāloka with Locana*, in Hindi by Acarya Jagannath Pathak, p. 193, Varanasi: Chowkhamba Vidyabhavan, 1965, henceforth *Dhvanyāloka (with Locana)*.

with the association of *rajas* and *tamas*. In other words, one can enjoy the taste of his own blissful consciousness or self due to the prominence of *sattva* quality. When there is prominence of *sattva*, it may provide a real mental repose (*viśrānti*). From this it does not follow that other qualities, i.e. *rajas* and *tamas*, are not there. The prominence of *sattva* quality along with the association of others in a non-prominence stage gives rise to the taste of own self as bliss-generating aesthetic pleasure. It is the aesthetic pleasure which only can do this thing. This joy is endowed with such type of mystic power by which the audience can enjoy this bliss even out of painful situation, but in our practical life human nature is found averse to the experience of pain (*evam hi sati tadduḥkhena so'pi duḥkhita iti kṛtvā rasasyātmateti niravakāśam bhavet*).[10] This pain is an impersonal one, but not personal. Had it been personal, the experience of pain would have arisen in the sage himself. Personal pain makes a man crippled while impersonal pain empowers him in creativity (*nirmāṇa-kṣamatva*). This empowerment through impersonal pain leads Vālmīki to create a poetry:

> *mā niṣāda pratiṣṭhām tvamāgamaḥ śāśvatīḥ samāḥ* ।
> *yat krauñcamithunādekamavadhīḥ kāmamohitam* ॥

> That is, Oh Fowler, you will never receive establishment in your life, as you have killed one of the pair of cranes who were engaged in sexual pleasure.

Hence, Viśvanātha, the celebrated rhetorician, has said that poetry is a peculiarly unworldly phenomenon, an extraordinary creation of supernatural supernormal genius and hence it cannot be governed by the rules of ordinary human intellect. In ordinary life sorrow arises from sorrow, fear follows fear, but in the world of poetry we find pleasure deriving from the painful, horrible and terrible situations.

> *hetutvam śokaharṣādergatebhyo lokasaṁśrayāt śokaharṣadayo loke jāyantam nāma laukikah* । *Alaukikavibhāvatvam prāptebhyaḥ kāvya-saṁśrayāt sukham sañjāyate tebhyaḥ sarvebhyo 'piti' kā kṣatiḥ* ॥
>
> — *Sāhityadarpaṇa*, 3.6-7

---

[10] *Dhvanyāloka with Locana*, p. 88.

Optics is the branch of Physics which involves the behaviour and properties of light including its interactions with matter. Optics usually describes the behaviour of visible, ultraviolet and infrared light. For, light is an electromagnetic wave other forms of electromagnetic radiations such as X-ray, microwaves and radiowaves exhibit similar properties.[11] In fact, the glory of light is always admitted both in physics and philosophy.

Optical physics is the study of matter–matter and light–matter interactions on the scale of single atom and molecules. Optical physics tends to focus on the fundamental properties of optical fields and their interactions with matter to the microscopic realm.

The main source of light on earth is the sun. Sunlight provides us energy that green plants use to create sugar mostly in the form of starches, which release energy in the living things that digest them. This process of photosynthesis provides virtually all the energy used by living things.

The Indian philosophers also believe that optics or light or energy remains in matter. When energy is found in water, trees, even garbage, it is called *vāravānala* (hydel power), *dāvānala* (energy received from forest trees) and power from garbage respectively. The power remaining in different material objects has to be extracted from them. In modern physics it is admitted that the sunlight gives energy to the green plants. Plants give more sugar which again releases energy for the living beings. Energy in human body can help our body to associate it with the power of digesting. In Indian philosophy four types of energy is admitted – divine energy (*divya teja*), worldly energy (*bhauma teja*), energy remaining in our stomach (*udaraja teja*) and energy of the matters remaining in mine (*ākāraja teja*).[12] The energy remaining in stomach is responsible for our digestion. The place where

---

[11] *McGraw-Hill Encyclopedia of Science and Technology* (5th edn), McGraw-Hill, 1993.

[12] *viṣayaścaturvidhau bhauma-divya-udarya-ākāraja-bhedāt* । *bhaumam vahnyādikam* । *avibandhanam divyam bidyudādi* । *bhuktasya pariṇāmahetuḥ udāryam* । *ākārajam suvarṇādi*. – *Tarkasaṁgraha* with *Dīpikā*, tr. Aurobindo Basu, p. 58, Kolkata: Mitram, 2010.

this energy remains for digestion of food is called *pākasthalī* (the place where something is being cooked or digested). If there is less energy which is not sufficient for appropriate digestion, it is called *agnimāndya* (weakened digestive fire) in the stomach (*jaṭharāgni*) due to the less flow of digestive juice. The disease is medically called dyspepsia. In the *Śrīmadbhagavadgītā* and the *Manu Saṁhitā* the science of optics is also eulogized. It is said that light of the sun gives rise to the accumulation of rain through evaporation and rain in return provides us eatable crops through which human beings can survive in this world (*ādityajjāyate vṛṣṭiḥ vṛṣṭerannam tataḥ prajāḥ*).[13] The rains again come down in this earth through downpour producing bumper crops (*annādbhavati bhūtāni parjanyādannasambhavaḥ*).[14] It is known from the above that there is a chain system in nature which starts with the science of light. This light is always taken as a metaphor signifying freedom or liberation or any form of relief while the state of bondage is symbolized as darkness as evidenced in the Upaniṣadic statement: *tamaso mā jyotirgamaya*.

From the above it is known to us that there is a chain system for protection of environment particularly the protection of plants and living things. Through the same light and energy *Prakṛti*'s *sattva* element overpowers the other constituents, *rajas* and *tamas*, and allows us to have goodwill to protect the whole environment after reducing anger and greed from us.

Like Vaiśeṣikas the physicists believe in five elements or matters like earth (*kṣiti*), water (*ap*), light (*tejas*), air (*marut*) and space (*ākāśa*). Vallabhācārya, a great philosopher in Indian tradition, in his *Nyāyalīlāvatī* has glorified earth (*kṣiti*) having weight (*gurutva*). As an earthly object has got some weight, it is natural that it will be drowned in water. But Vallabha is of the opinion that there is a tendency in certain object to float or to come to the surface of water without going inside water due to having some sort of impediment on the way of drowning (*jalādhogamanam jalena dhāraṇam patanaprativandhonmajjanam, etacca jalasya yogasya*

[13] *Manu Saṁhitā* 3.76.

[14] *Śrīmadbhagavadgītā* 3.14.

kasyacideva patanaprativandhasamarthyāt).[15] Vallabha talks of a particular resistance to sinking or gravity exercised by water, which explains the tendency in certain objects to float or to come up to the surface of water. Vallabha was perhaps not aware of the formula of Archimedes at that time which tells that body loses its weight if immersed in water and the weight it loses is equivalent to weight of the volume of water displaced by it.

The five essential elements for the protection of our body are also mentioned in the *Caraka Saṁhitā*. The roughness, liquidity, moving force, vital force and vacuum of the body are gathered from the physical elements like *kṣiti* and *ap*.[16] It is also mentioned that all the above-mentioned characters of human body are easily understood with the help of tactual sense organ (*lakṣaṇam sarvamaitat sparśanendriyagocaraḥ*).[17]

First, let us suppose that space and time are continuous. Zeno presents two paradoxes to show that, on this supposition, motion is impossible. The Racetrack Imagine that we are trying to move from point *A* to point *B*. Suppose *C* is the midpoint of the distance from *A* to *B*. It seems that we have to first get from *A* to *C*, before we can get from *A* to *B*. Now suppose that *D* is the midpoint between *A* and *C*; just as above, it seems that we have to first get from *A* to *D* before we can get from *A* to *C*. Since space is infinitely divisible, this process can be continued indefinitely. So it seems that you need to complete an infinite series of journeys before you can travel any distance – even a very short one! *A* flying arrow, according to Zeno, is at rest, i.e. occupying equal space.[18]

In the like manner, the Naiyāyikas have shown a paradox in the concept of time (*kāla*). It is defined as the cause of verbal usage of the past, etc. is called time (*kāla*). It is said in the *Bhāṣāpariccheda* by Viśvanātha that time has to be accepted as a producer of the

---

[15] *Positive Sciences*, p. 185.

[16] *Caraka Samhitā* XXVI.

[17] Ibid., chap. I.

[18] W.E. Abraham, 1972, "The Nature of Zeno's Argument Against Plurality in DK 29 B I", *Phronesis*, 17: 40-52.

effects and as the substratum of the universe (*janyānām jahakaḥ kālo jagarāmāśrayo mataḥ*).[19] In a word, the auxiliary cause of any type of effect (*kāryamātram*) is called time.[20] Because, the usages like "Today a jar will be produced" (*adya ghaṭo bhaviṣyati*), "Yesterday a jar was produced" (*śvaḥ ghaṭo bhavitā*), etc. are possible due to the acceptance of time as the cause of the origination of such effects, and also as the cause of the origination of such awareness expressed in language.[20]

In the foregoing discussion some paradoxes and defects may be shown in their arguments given by the Naiyāyikas.

First, if time were defined in terms of the cause of the usages like past and present, there would arise the defect of circularity or fallacy of mutual dependence (*anyonyāśraya*). For, time is understood in terms of the usages like past, while the usages like past, are understood in terms of time.

Second, it is very difficult to define past, present and future on account of the fact that there is "no cut-off time" in comparison to which an object is said to be existing in past or present. An incident occurred a moment before, may be taken as past and that occurred one hundred years back is also called past. What is the exact time that we can call "present" and in terms of which past and future may be determined? It is very difficult to determine a span of time, which we call "present". The Buddhists would say that an incident occurring in a particular moment is present, but it is beyond conceptualization. It would take more than one moment to conceptualize "present", and hence the question of past and future does not arise at all. Therefore, time defined as above is paradoxical.

If the "present" (*vartamāna*) is not determined, the "past" (*atīta*) remains undetermined. Because, the absenteeness existing in an

---

[19] *Bhāṣāpariccheda*, verse 45.

[20] *adya ghaṭo bhaviṣyati, śvah paṭo bhavitā ityārdipratītestattatkāryotpattya-dhikaraṇatvena vyavahāraviṣayasya tasya kālasya tattadutpattihetutvāt . . .* – *Muktāvalīsaṁgraha* on verse 45, by Panchanan Bhattacharya, p. 201, Calcutta, 1374 (BS).

absentee of the destruction occurred at the "present" is called "pastness" (*atītatva*) (*vartamānakālavṛttidhvaṁśa-pratiyogitvama atītatvam*). In other words, the absentee of destruction existing in the present (*vartamāna*) is called "past". In the same way, the absenteeness existing in an absentee of the prior-absence occurred in the "present" time is the futureness (*anāgatatva*) (*vartamānakālavṛtti-prāgabhāva-prātiyogitvam anāgatatvam*). In other words, something whose prior absence remains in the "present" is called future (*anāgata*).[21]

As Zeno has shown paradoxes in space and time, the Naiyāyikas have shown paradoxes in conceptualizing time.

---

[21] *atītatvam vartamānakālāvṛttidhvaṁśapratiyogitvam* ı *anāgatatvam vartamānakālavṛttiprāgabhāvapratiyogitvam* – *Nirukti* on *Tarkasaṁgraha*, ed. Satkari Sharma Bangiya, p. 19, Varanasi: Chowkhamba, 1976.

7

Zero : An Eternal Enigma

Parthasarathi Mukhopadhyay

SUPPOSE you have two pens and I take one of those from you. How many pens do you have now? Of course, your answer will be "one". Suppose further that I take the remaining pen from you as well. Now if I ask you again the same question as before, sure enough, you will say "none at all"! But observe that, while answering to an affirmative question, you chose to give a negative answer not by a number but through language! However, if you want to give an affirmative answer in this case, the number that you require is "zero", the greatest gift of India to the world, without which the present prosperity of modern civilizations through various scientific achievements would never have been possible, so says many a great historian of science.

Though the exact timeframe of its origin is hotly debated, it is generally accepted worldwide that the decimal (i.e. base ten) system of enumeration along with the number "zero" (0) of our present day, was first thought of in ancient India, both philosophically and mathematically. It originated from the Sanskrit word *śūnya*, which was only one of the several synonyms used to represent the concept. One of its roles is that of a placeholder, where it allows the digits from 1 to 9 to take their own "places" in the decimal representation, so as to be able to distinguish between, say 12 and 10002. With passage of time, it eventually became an independent numeral, a number in its own right, for mathematical expression of "nothing", as we use it today while writing $2 - 2 = 0$.

We, the educated Indians, are in general aware of the fact that in some remote past, Indian mathematicians discovered the number "zero", as is usually mentioned in our school books. Some even mention, though erroneously, that Āryabhaṭa discovered zero! But what really is meant by this "discovery"? Neither was it invented in a laboratory, nor excavated from somewhere! How did the ancients manage without zero, before the so-called discovery? How could they distinguish between, say, 101 and 100001? Why that method is not being followed now?

Apart from India, there were various other glorious ancient civilizations that scaled fantastic heights in a variety of fields including mathematics. What were their enumeration systems? Did they know about "zero" as a number in its own right or at least as a concept representing void or nothingness? If any of these civilizations at all had the concept of some kind of "zero", why their "zero" is not considered today as the forefather of our modern "zero"? To know these answers from the proper perspective, one has to scan a rich history of various early civilizations through a period of over 5,000 years. In this engaging tour of sociocultural history, the journey takes us through the Egyptian hieroglyphics, via Babylonian clay tablets and grotesque looking Mayan glyphs, the ingenious Inca *quipu*, followed by the great Greek civilization and the mighty Roman empire in the West, whereas we come to know about the lofty philosophy of void by ancient Indian seers along with their incredible mathematical achievements, clever Chinese enumeration system and industrious pursuits of wise Arabians of Baghdad in the East. Told with due rigour, this would explode to an epic proportion, for which this is perhaps not the right place. Hence, touching each of these facets, if only tangentially, let us try to place in a nutshell, the true genesis of modern "zero" in its proper historical footing – an ode to the *Nothing – That Is*!

Egypt

Egyptians (about 3000 BCE), in their enumeration system, never used any symbol or concept like "zero" as a number in its own right. However, at a later stage of their civilization, they have sometimes used the hieroglyph *n f r* (which literally means "beautiful") to indicate the base or ground level reference line towards constructing the higher base level of some of the pyramids to save the inner burial chamber from almost routine inundation by River Nile. From this base level they would measure the length in cubits (an unit of length, from tip of the elbow to that of the stretched fingers) both in upward and downward directions for the construction of the pyramid. Though they gave a definite importance to the numerical symbol for "ten" and its higher powers in their hieroglyphic enumeration system, their representation of a number was additive in nature, in the sense that the values of the numerical symbols written side by side were to be added to understand the number represented by them.

Babylon [Akkadian]

"Zero" in the sense of a placeholder (which looked like a "double wedge" sign, somewhat like two partially overlapping < one on top of the other) was used from around fourth century BCE in Babylonia in their sexagesimal (i.e. base sixty, where two numerical symbols for "one" written side-by-side does not mean "1 times 10 + 1 = eleven", rather it means "1 times sixty + 1 = sixty-one") system of enumeration, as found in their numerous clay tablets, though the Babylonians never thought of this "zero" as a number in its own right, as ancient Indians regularly did, though we do not have any direct written evidence due to the oral tradition that prevailed then. Before their invention of this "double wedge" sign for "zero" to fill up the vacant place in a number, Babylonians used to leave a gap in the requisite number to represent occurrence(s) of zero. But that only added to the confusion. For example, in modern notations, if we write 11 and 1 1, can we be sure of how many zeros are to be inserted in the gap of the second number to understand it? This situation prevailed in Babylonia for over a thousand years, before some Babylonian genius came to understand that a gap-filling symbol is necessary to overcome this problem. This symbol may be considered as the oldest known symbol for *placeholder zero* in human civilization.

Mexico [Maya]

The Mayans of Mexico (200 BCE – 1540 CE) used the number "zero" in their vigesimal system (i.e. base twenty, in which two numerical symbols for "one" written side-by-side does not mean "1 times 10 + 1 = eleven", rather it means "1 times twenty + 1 = twenty-one"; and by the way, Mayans used to write numbers, not side-by-side but from top-to-bottom with the same interpretation). Their "zero" was not a mere placeholder, indeed it was a pure number in its own right. They had five different symbols or glyphs to represent their "zero", one of which, the most common one, being a red-coloured seashell. They developed some very advanced calendars for keeping time. In one of these calendars (called *Haab*) they had 18 months (called *winal*) with 20 days (called *kin*) in each of them, (followed by a phantom month *Uayeb* of five days, to make up for their year, a *tun*), where the beginning day of each month was reckoned as the day zero and not day one! But still we cannot call their "zero" as the forefather of our present "zero", since it lacks certain fundamental mathematical features as can be seen from their Long Count calendar. In this calendar Mayans kept record of their important historical events, by first counting the total number of days that has elapsed since their own understanding of Day Zero (13 August 3114 BCE, with respect to our modern calendar) which was, according to them, the day of creation of the Universe. Then they used to subdivide this total number of days (*kin*) into several higher units of time, like month (*winal* = 20 *kin*), year (*tun* = 18 *winal*), and even further, much higher units like *katun* (= 20 *tun*), *baktun* (= 20 *katun*), etc. and engraved them on a stone, now known as a stella. However, trying to keep the number of days in a year as close to the actual number 365 as possible, which seemed to be their priority of purpose, they had unknowingly destroyed the arithmetical pattern of base 20 place value system by putting 18 times 20 in the third place (1 *tun* = 18 times 20 *kin*, i.e. 360 *kin*), instead of mathematically required 20 times 20. This induced a serious drawback to the mathematical property of their "zero" in an otherwise brilliant vigesimal place value system. A truly commensurate "zero" in a properly organized place value system, when sits to the right of a given number, must refer to the number which is "11" times the original, where "*n*" is the base of that place value system. For example, in decimal (base 10) system, when we write 120 by putting a 0 to the right of 12, it becomes

10 times 12 in value, or in binary (base 2) system, 110 (which stands for the decimal number 6), is 2 times 11 (which stands for the decimal number 3), similarly in ternary (base 3) system, 110 (which now stands for the decimal number 12), is 3 times 11 (which now stands for the decimal number 4), etc. Observe that according to the Mayan long count, their numeral "one zero zero" became representative of 360 (i.e. 1 into 18 times 20) rather than 400 (i.e. 1 into 20 times 20), as would have been the case in a correct vigesimal system. Hence their "zero" cannot be considered as the true predecessor of our modern mathematical "zero".

Peru [Inca]

The Incas (around 1500 CE) ruled Peru with brilliant arithmetical efficiency, though there was no written language at that time. However, a rigorous record keeping of taxes received, etc. was calculated and preserved through specially knotted strings called *Quipu*, a large number of which can be seen nowadays at various Natural History museums worldwide. It was a decimal (i.e. base ten) place value representation of numbers, where placeholder "zero" was represented by keeping a gap at the required place on the string.

China

Early Chinese civilization used a multiplicative–additive system, based on written decimal place value symbols put within successive digits with a special sign to represent absence of a digit in certain place, if necessary. For example, to write 13, they would write, from left to right, their symbol for one followed by that of ten and then put the symbol for three. Later they started calculating with the "rod numerals", made with small bumboo sticks, an early form of abacus, where much like the Babylonians, a gap was used to represent zero (which they called "Kong"). From around eighth century CE, Chinese got the idea of filling up this gap, as some leading experts believe (Gupta 2015) from a Buddhist monk of India, Gotama Siddha by name, and started using "zero", which was denoted by a thick dot (called *bindu* in Sanskrit). But of course there are other, minority views, arguing in favour of Chinese claim of origin of the concept of mathematical zero, as one may find in a relatively recent work by Meera Nanda (2016). She argues that the mathematical concept of zero originated actually in mainland China and it got transmitted through traders and mingled with Indian shape of circular looking zero somewhere at the Sino-Indian cross-cultural border regions of the then Buddhist Cambodia. However, an interesting point by point refutation of many of her claims may also be found in the article by Michel Danino (2016).

Greece

Much earlier, Greek mathematicians from fifth century BCE were fascinated with Geometry and the concept of ratio among numbers, and thereby developed a fear and hatred of the number "zero", as it threatened to destroy their much-cherished concept of ratio-based understanding of the perception of beauty in the universe, as the ratio of a number with "zero" is mathematically incomprehensible. So Pythagoreans, while hailed the dictum "All is number", discarded "zero" as a number. For them, every number must have a shape, which can be created on the ground by arranging as many pebbles suitably, like triangular numbers (e.g. 1, 3, 6, 10), square numbers (e.g. 1, 4, 9, 16), pentagonal numbers (e.g. 1, 5, 12, 22), hexagonal numbers (e.g. 1, 6, 15, 28), etc. They raised the question, "if zero means nothing, how can *nothing* be represented by *something*? After all, what shape can nothing have?" Moreover, Greek philosopher Aristotle had declared "Nature abhors a vacuum". He was very influential in the society as he had given a "proof" of existence of God, by declaring Him as the *Prime Mover*, responsible personally for moving the seventh, i.e. the outermost celestial sphere, harbouring the seventh planet Saturn, as per their understanding of geocentric universe at that time. So Greeks decided that there was no zero and no infinity, everything in the universe must be finite. This unfortunate dictum, which kept the great Archimedes from almost discovering Integral Calculus about two millennia before its time, was then to be followed for about two thousand years in Europe, as Catholic Church at a later date accepted the Aristotelian doctrine. In due course of time, contesting Aristotle was tantamount to challenging the authority of the church, which in the Middle Age Europe could easily cost one's life, even by being burnt alive at stake. Greek enumeration system was additive in nature and there were no separate numeral symbols; their alphabets written with a bar on top used to represent numbers, where the largest number was only ten thousand, called *miryori*, denoted by the letter *M*. At a later period, Hellenistic astronomers, while recording the angular positions of the celestial bodies, extended their alphabetic numerals into a base 60 positional system, much like the Babylonians, by limiting each position to a maximum value of 59 and including a special symbol for zero, which looked like an "o with a bar or dumb-bell on top", believed to have come from the first letter of the Greek word *Ouden* meaning "nothing". However, in the usual Greek alphabetic numeral system, this "o", called "*omicron*", stood for seventy! The Hellenistic zero was also used alone like our modern zero, more than as a simple placeholder. However, the positions were limited to the fractional part of a number (called minutes, seconds, thirds, fourths, etc.) – it was not used in the integral *degree* part of a number. This system was probably adapted from Babylonian numerals by Hipparchus *c*.140 BCE. It was then used by the Greek astronomers of Alexandria like Ptolemy (*c*.140 CE) who backed the Aristotelian view of geocentric universe, Theon (*c*.380 CE) and Theon's daughter, Hypatia (who was brutally murdered in 415 CE on a street of Alexandria by a Roman mob as a result of her refusal to adopt Christian religious faith).

Rome

Thanks to Ptolemaic school of fortune telling, by this time most of the mathematician–astronomers were fortune tellers as well, and were generally hated in the society, as many of their predictions failed to match the reality. Primarily engaged in politicking and military expansions, the mighty Romans (27 BCE – 1453 CE) never thought mathematics worthy of much attention. In Roman numeral system, to understand the meaning of a numerical symbol, one has to add, or sometime even has to subtract, the values of the respective individual symbols put side by side. For example, when the symbols V for 5 and I for 1 are put side by side as VI, it stands for 5 + 1, i.e. 6, but when you write IV it means 5 – 1, i.e. 4. However in this clumsy system, though C stands for 100, IC does not stand for 100 – 1, i.e. 99, for which you have to write XCIX, which depicts the number as ten (X) less than hundred and nine (IX) added to it! One can easily imagine the Herculean effort or specialist expertise that is needed to simply multiply or divide numbers written in this system. This system requires no "zero" as a placeholder, but more and more new symbols are to be introduced in the system for representing larger numbers. And since there is no "largest" number, so the requirement for newer symbols become unlimited! Famous historian A.L. Basham in his book, *The Wonder That Was India*, has aptly pointed out:

> Most of the great discoveries and inventions of which Europe is so proud would have been impossible without a developed system of mathematics, and this in turn would have been impossible if Europe had been shackled by the unwieldy system of Roman numerals. The unknown man who devised the new system was from the world's point of view, after the Buddha, the most important son of India. His achievement, though easily taken for granted, was the work of an analytic mind of first order. ..."

India

Historical reconstruction of mathematical knowledge, that was likely to be prevalent in Indian antiquity, is much like arranging an enormous jigsaw puzzle, many pieces of which are missing. Competent historians of Mathematics, all over the world, are trying to rearrange the available pieces, according to their own respective stances, with an obvious intention to try and guess the picture it may suggest. And the job is anything but linear. Patriotic passion and pre-conceived ideas often come in the way of scholarly acumen, prompting one to misplace, perhaps subconsciously, one or two pieces here and there, or may be not to place them at all, distorting the figure to accommodate one's "stance", not to mention the most unfortunate intrusion of one's personal political ideological belief. Some have decided a priori to make the picture look like the dancing Śiva, while few others seem to be determined to find a dancing monkey instead! Of course, there is a third group, carefully steering a discrete middle course, analysing objectively as far as possible, the available pieces of evidence or information and sometimes even the lack of information, trying to make a logically conceivable pattern out of it, with every new piece being found occasionally, as a new input to the jigsaw puzzle, one has to try and find its right place in the puzzle, sometimes destroying the existing pattern. And the journey continues.

The genesis of "zero", a number that even a child so casually uses today, is a long and involved one. A good number of experts concerned with the history of its evolution, today accept that the number zero, in its true potential, as we use it in modern mathematics, has its root, conceptually as well as etymologically, in the word *śūnya* of Indian antiquity. However, the exact timeframe of its origin is still hotly debated. Furthermore, as we have already mentioned, some researchers try to suggest that a trace of this concept, if not in total operational perspective, might have had a Greek origin that travelled to India during the Greek invasion of the northern part of our country in the pre-Mauryan period. According to them, the "decimal place-value principle with zero as a hallmark", was in actuality not an independent Indian achievement. The root of it presumably lies with the Babylonians (Akkadians), who by 300 BCE had started using a queer symbol of two slanted wedges to denote an empty placemark in a written numeral on unbaked clay tablets, instead of keeping a "blank space", as they had been doing before, for over a thousand years. Though these historians seem to give some concession to the decimal place-value system in favour of India, which according to them "was being employed in India, especially among the Jainas and Buddhists, towards the beginning of the common era", as far as the inception of "zero" and its symbol is concerned, they opine to the contrary. Laying an undue stress on the "symbol" part of it, they claim that Greek (astronomical) Papyri of the period immediately preceding and following the beginning of the common era demonstrate that, they filled (the blank space) with an adaptation of the Akkadian symbol for zero (two slanted wedges); this adaptation looks like a circle with a bar over it.

Earlier, this sign, often referred to as the "Hellenistic zero", used by astronomers like Ptolemy and some of his successors, only in the fractional part of a sexagesimal number (called minutes, seconds, third, fourth, etc.) and not in the integral part, was thought to have emerged out of the first letter "omicron" of the Greek word *ouden*, meaning nothing. However O. Neugebaur dismissed this claim by pointing out the fact that *omicron* was already used to mean 70 according to the Greek alphabetic enumeration system.

Some other scholars like Robert Kaplan (2000) argue that possibly it came from *obol*, a contemporary coin of almost no value. They conjecture that the typical round sign evolved during the use of counters in sand-boards for arithmetical calculation. The impression left on sand when such a counter was removed to leave an empty column, perhaps gave birth to the symbol as a circle. Further arguments amount to the claim that, after the invasion of northern India, the Greeks came to India in large numbers, brought with them documents with such a symbol written there and while translating these documents into Sanskrit (with which the Indian mathematicians/astronomers like Varāhamihira are credited), the symbol for zero was taken as a circle (*pūrṇa*), the full moon, or a dot (*bindu*). The earliest such incident, according to David Pingree (Ifrah 2000), took place around 425 CE, the principal impetus behind the whole theory being "there is no certain evidence that a symbol for zero was in place (in India) before the fifth century AD". These viewpoints however do not explain why the Greek mathematicians did not or could not use this so-called "zero" to the full mathematical potential. Due to their geographical location, they were the natural inheritors of Babylonian place value system; yet even after they were exposed to this more powerful system of enumeration, they apparently failed to judge the power of it, used it only in astronomical calculation, and that too not freely and arithmetically stuck to their own clumsy system of enumeration. Why is it that the genius of Archimedes or the galaxy of Greek geometrical giants could not recognize it? Some believe that it was perhaps due to their overemphasis on geometric ideas, trying to interpret the universe in tandem with their Pythagorean perception of geometry, and this perception did not approve of the concept of "zero" as a number. Or was it the Aristotelian dictum – *Nature abhors vacuum* – that stood in their way, raising a philosophical conundrum like "how can nothing be represented by something?".

Leo Depuydt (2008), a noted historian of antiquity, observes: "History is, by definition, the period for which we have written sources." Going by such a definition, one may easily be tempted to reach a conclusion as:

> Our current numbering system is Indian in origin and took shape during the period of cultural and intellectual splendour that took place along the valley of the Ganges from the mid-third century to the mid-fourth century CE. During this period, the Gupta dynasty reigned the region.

However, this definition cannot be of much help and needs to be taken with a pinch of salt, if one were to trace the genesis of mathematical knowledge in Indian antiquity, particularly in the pre-Christian era, perhaps dating back to several millennia further, owing to the complete unavailability of written documents pertaining to this period. Though, from the huge collection of available documents of later dates beginning from the early Christian era, where one may find regular references to ancient works of amazingly lofty philosophical thoughts, mingled with occasional flashes of extraordinary scientific sophistication, it goes without saying that the remote antiquity in India cradled a civilization of a very high order. The mathematical heritage of the Indian subcontinent has long been recognized to be extremely rich. Hundreds of thousands of manuscripts in India and elsewhere, mostly written in Sanskrit, attest to this tradition. It is with this background of the social context and ambiance of the Indian antiquity in mind that one must try to judge the possible potential mathematical developments, as testified passively by various apparently non-mathematical resources, in case of the absence of direct mathematical testimony. The philosophical concept of *śūnya* and the Sanskrit words akin to it, in their broader social and philosophical contexts, might eventually pave the way for the evolution of the corresponding mathematical concept of zero.

In ancient India, much unlike Greece, philosophers of every school of thoughts seemed to have toyed freely with the concept of vacuum and investigated it inquisitively. In the Tantra, one finds the eternal divine creator Niṣkala Śiva, the undifferentiated formless emancipation of the God Śiva, who creates this whole universe from void and destroys his creation into the void again and again. From the Nasadīya Sūkta of the *Ṛgveda*, where the Vedic seers are philosophically trying to imagine the nature of the vacuum before the creation of the universe, to the Śūnyavāda or doctrine of devoidness of the philosopher Nāgārjuna from Mahāyāna school of Buddhism, where the highest form of knowledge, i.e. *prajñāpāramitā* is attributed to the perception of everything phenomenal or worldly as *śūnya*, the pure void, and attaining this state of mind is defined as the *nirvāṇa*, it appears very likely that the thread of rich philosophical and socio-academic ambiances of Indian antiquity was quite pregnant with the immensity of the concept of *śūnya* – a dichotomy as well as a simultaneity between "nothing" and "everything", the *śūnya* (zero) of void and that of an all-pervading fathomless *pūrṇa* (infinite). In this society, when mathematicians declared the necessity of having a numeral for *śūnya*, the society at large never contradicted the idea or tried to resist it, as was the case in Greece. One may find several decimal nomenclatures in the *Ṛgveda*, a reference to the number zero as *kṣudra* in the *Atharvaveda* as well. However, the most common parlance for zero in ancient India was *kha*, which literally means the sky, also referred to as *śūnya*. This Sanskrit word is derived from *suna* [+ *yat*], which is the past participle of the root *svi*, which means "to swell" or "to grow", and therefrom by semantic extension "hollow".

In the *Ṛgveda*, one may find another meaning "the sense of lack or deficiency". The two different meanings were fused to give *śūnya* a single sense of absence or emptiness with the potential for growth, a womb-like hollow, ready to swell. Early reference to zero is found in the *Gopatha Brāhmaṇa* as *chidra* (a puncture mark) or as *randhra* (a hole), in the *Amarakoṣa*, or as *śūnya-bindu* (zero dot), in the drama the *Vāsavadattā* by Subandhu (*c.*400 CE) which clearly refers to the possible shape or form of it, as was thought of at those time. Ifrah (2000) has given a reference of a Jaina cosmological text the *Lokabibhāga* (458 CE) with concrete example of zero being used as a placeholder. Another Jaina work the *Anujogadvarasūtra* of first century CE also reveals clear understanding of placeholder zero in a decimal place value system. Indeed, such list is too large to discuss here comprehensively (Mukhopadhayay 2009).

In the early Vedic society, veneration for Sanskrit exalted it as sacred speech – *devabhāṣa* – whose divinely revealed texts were meant to be recited, heard and memorized collectively rather than transmitted in writing. Naturally it gave rise to the necessity that such texts be composed in formats that could be easily memorized. It was done in two modes, either through condensed prose aphorisms, called *sūtra*s or in verse form, particularly in the classical period, beginning in the late first millennium BCE. Analysing the reasons behind the abundance of metrical verse-based resources of Indian antiquity and the consequent indispensable need for careful and systematic analysis of poetic metrics, A.K. Dutta (2009) concludes:

> Ancient Indians had the perception that the metrical form has greater durability, power, intensity and force than the unmetrical, and hence recorded all important knowledge in verse form.

The Vedic seers attributed almost mystic significance to *chandas*, consequently, close attention was paid to the study of Chandaḥśāstra, i.e. the science of verse metres. Since no written mathematical treatise of remote Indian antiquity is extant, historians have turned their attention to the non-mathematical texts of that period, with an intention to find tacit mathematical clues, if there be any. The idea is to dig deep into the academic ambience of that period and analyse in the light of those works, the available social contexts, towards a possible unearthing of some threads of mathematical thought, which might have been prevalent during that period. If non-mathematicians are found to be at ease with novel mathematical concepts, for example, that of "zero" as a digit in its own right, in an arguably place-value system, it certainly strengthens the argument in favour of those people doing *gaṇita* in that society, to have already mastered those concepts. Two such cases are certainly worth mentioning, one directly referring to the number "zero" of mathematics and the other tacitly applying a similar concept of placeholder.

In this regard, the *Piṅgalacchandaḥsūtra*, the rules of prosody for both Vedic and classical *chanda* given by Piṅgala, arguably sometime during second century BCE, come into the limelight as an irrefutable landmark in the history of mathematics, particularly in connection with the priority in the inception of place-value notation, as in two of its *sūtra*s, it formally mentions the term *śūnya* as a clear mathematical concept of "zero", for the first time in the history of human civilization (as far as our present evidences stand), and discusses formulations for intricate combinatorial calculations towards, thanks to Van Nooten (1993), what is now recognized as binary arithmetic, going up to conversion of a decimal number to binary and vice versa – an extraordinary feat indeed. After a critical examination of all the 315 *sūtra*s spread over the eight chapters of his work, one finds the *sūtra*s 20-35 in the eighth chapter to be of immense mathematical potential. As usual, they are in keeping with the spirit of pithy and cryptic presentation of a *sūtra*, almost obscure to a non-specialist. However, thanks to the later commentaries, they can be relatively easily deciphered to produce an excellent account of combinatorial calculation as has been shown in details by S.R. Sarma (2003) among others. The *sūtra*s 28-31 deal with the combinatorial question: *How many different meters are there with a given length*? That is, to compute the total number of possible arrangements of "long" and "short" syllables (respectively, the *guru* and the *laghu*), repetition allowed, without actually constructing the arrangement of all possible combinations of *guru* and *laghu* in a given metre (called the *prastara*, a bed or matrix in which the *guru*s and *laghu*s are listed horizontally). The *sūtra*s 29 and 30, *rūpeśūnyam* and *dviḥśūnye* by name, clearly mention the term *śūnya*. However to see them work as mathematical "zero", one has to combine them along with the *sūtra*s immediately preceding and immediately succeeding them, viz. *dvirardhe* and *tavadardhe tadguṇitam*. Four of them, put together in a row, and interpreted according to the commentators, give us the necessary rule of computation which clearly involves a notion of modern mathematical "zero". Of course, wherever Piṅgala had referred to *śūnya*, he did it in language and not by any symbol. So whatever symbol for *śūnya* he might have had in his mind remains beyond us. But, his choice favouring the term *śūnyam* clearly indicates that during his time, a concept of mathematical *śūnya* was prevalent. Van Nooten (1993) observes that "we can be reasonably certain that his counting system was predicated on a base of ten". He further points out that a system of notation that simply uses two symbols as markers of a place value does not necessarily produce a binary system. But if there is a system that uses two symbols in such a way that every string made with them has a unique decimal equivalent and it is shown how one may convert a decimal number into a string of those two symbols uniquely, then "indeed we do have a binary system. Piṅgala has done at least this much". In the view of Needham and Ling (1959):

> Place value could and did exist without any symbol for zero. But zero symbol as a part of the numerical system never existed and could not have come into being without place-value.

Along this line of argument S.R. Sarma (2003) concluded that

> the invention of decimal place-value system along with the concept and symbol of zero must antedate considerably Piṅgala's mention of the zero symbol.

Passion for attaining perfection in grammar, recognized as a Vedāṅga, was of paramount importance in the Vedic studies in ancient India. Pāṇini, the great grammarian of arguably seventh century BCE, author of the *Aṣṭādhyāyī*, an archetypal work thoroughly systematizing the Sanskrit grammar, exhibited extraordinary technical and descriptive skills.

Researches deep into the analysis of the Pāṇinian grammar, which has an inherent scientific "structure", have been carried out by many scholars, both Indian and Western. One of them, from recent times, F. Staal (2010) opines that Pāṇini's use of his grammatical or linguistic "zero", viz. *lopa*, was used as a marker of an empty (*śūnya*) or non-occupied space or position. His relevant basic *sūtra* is *adarśanam lopaḥ*, found in the *Aṣṭādhyāyī* (I.1.60) which means "non-appearance is *lopa*", a concept which can be rendered by the modern term "zeroing". In this regard Bloomfield (1961) points out: "The Hindus hit upon the apparently artificial but in practice eminently serviceable device of speaking of a zero element." In a later elaborate work of truly seminal nature, viz. *Zero in Panini*, M.D. Pandit (1990) comments:

> The only technical principle that Pāṇini might have and has actually used is the principle of zero, which he perhaps borrowed from positional mathematics.

However, A.K. Dutta observes:

> One does not know whether the mathematical zero existed by his time and whether he was influenced by it, or whether it was Pāṇini's grammar which inspired the great mathematical invention.

But Pāṇini's techniques of linguistic analysis do consist of some basic fibres of abstract universality, making one feel that they are comparable to those adopted in mathematics.

In the context of the discussion made so far, interpretations by D. Pingree (2003) and the co-sharers of his opinion seem quite untenable. The thread of rich philosophical and socio-academic ambiances of Indian antiquity seems to be quite pregnant with the immensity of the concept of *śūnya*, a dichotomy as well as a simultaneity between nothing and everything, the "zero" of void and that of an all-pervading "fathomless" infinite. It therefore appears more probable that Indians, even in pre-common era, were familiar with the mathematical perspectives of *śūnya*. Whatever symbol for this concept they might have used or thought at that early stage is, of course, not known to us.

Arabia

It was during the reign of Abbasid Caliph Harun Al-Rashid (eighth century CE) that Arab scholars of Bayt-Al-Hikma (House of Wisdom) like Al-Khwarizmi from Baghdad took *śūnya* and other decimal numbers from Indian works like the *Brahmasphuṭasiddhānta* of Brahmagupta and gradually through their translation it was introduced to Europe after the Dark Age, from where it eventually got spread throughout the world in their Latin translations after fighting against a stubborn resistance of the Catholic Church for about five hundred years. Initially Church was dead against the use of decimal system with zero, as they considered it to be Arabic in origin, and hence anti-Christian. However, with the gradual fall of Aristotelianism, through the epoch-making scientific works of Galileo, Torricelli, Pascal in establishing sustained vacuum in nature, and that of Copernicus, Bruno, Kepler in establishing the heliocentric model of the universe contrary to the geocentric Aristotelian model backed by the Ptolemaic theory of epicycles, while mathematician René Descartes put the number zero practically in the centre stage of his *Coordinate Geometry* establishing that curves from Greek geometry and equations from Arabic algebra are really like opposite sides of the same coin, the Church had to finally back out. But that story is far too long to be told here in detail. Today these numbers are recognized worldwide as the Hindu–Arabic numerals.

We put an end to this story with a befitting remark once made by G.B. Halsted:

> The importance of the creation of the zero mark can never be exaggerated. This giving to airy nothing, not merely a local habitation and a name, a picture, a symbol, but helpful power, is the characteristic of the Hindu race from whence it sprang. . . . No single mathematical creation has been more potent for the general on-go of intelligence and power.

References

Bloomfield, L., 1961, *Language*, p. 132, New York: Holt Rinehart and Winston.

Danino, Michel, 2016, "In Defence of Indian Science", 13-14 October, *The New Indian Express*; \\http:www.newindianexpress.com/opinions/2016/oct/13/in-defence-of-indian-science-1527495-1.html

Depuydt, Leo, 2008, "Review of the Book: *Unexpected Links between Egyptian and Babylonian Mathematics* by J. Friberg", *The Mathematical Intelligencer*, 30(3): 72.

Dutta, Amartya Kumar, 2009, "Mathematics in Ancient India: Some Glimpses", in *Bharatatattva*, Kolkata: Ramakrishna Mission Institute of Culture.

Gupta, R.C., 2015, "Who Invented the Zero?", in *Ganitananda: Selected Works of R C. Gupta on History of Mathematics*, ed. K. Ramasubramanian, pp. 70-83.

Ifrah, G., 2000, *The Universal History of Numbers*, New York: John Wiley and Sons.

Kaplan, Robert, 2000, *The Nothing That Is: A Natural History of Zero*, New York: Oxford University Press.

Mukhopadhyay, Parthasarathi, 2009, "Concept of Sunya in Indian Antiquity", *Jour. Pure Math.*, 26: 15-49.

Nanda, Meera, 2016, *Science in Saffron: Skeptical Essays on History of Science*, Mohali: Indian Institute of Science Education & Research.

Needham, J. and Wang Ling, 1959, *Science and Civilization in China*, vol. II, p. 10, Cambridge: Cambridge University Press.

Pandit, M.D., 1990, *Zero in Panini*, Pune: University of Poona.

Pingree, David, 2003, "Zero and the Symbol for Zero in Early Sexagesimal and Decimal Place-Value Systems", in *The Concept of Sunya*, ed. A.K. Bag and S.R. Sarma, pp. 137-41, New Delhi: Aryan Books International.

Sarma, S.R., 2003, "Sunya in Pingala's Chandahsutra", in *The Concept of Sunya*, ed. A.K. Bag and S.R. Sarma, pp. 126-36, New Delhi: Aryan Books International.

Staal, Frits, 2010, "On the Origins of Zero: Studies in the History of Indian Mathematics", in *Culture and History of Mathematics*, vol. 5, pp. 39-53, Delhi: Hindustan Book Agency.

Van Nooten, B., 1993, "Binary Numbers in Indian Antiquity", *J. Indian Philosophy*, 21: 31-50.

8

Scientific Thoughts in Indian Philosophy

Sanjit Kumar Sadhukhan

IT IS absurd to think that the literature of a nation is totally free from scientific phenomena or thoughts or results. As the daily life is somehow effected by some scientific events, the literature must record them however scanty they may be. A poetical work may not record a scientific event or thought in a direct manner but a philosophical work more or less involves a regular and deep investigation in its subject matter, and as for which a philosophical work may sometimes be considered as an introductory science book. And it actually happened at least in the cases of Vaiśeṣika and Yoga schools of Indian philosophy. I would like to present the scientific thoughts in these two schools.

The nine main schools of Indian philosophy are divided into two broad sections: theistic and atheistic. Theistic section comprises six schools: Vedānta, Mīmāṁsā, Nyāya, Vaiśeṣika, Yoga and Sāṁkhya whereas the atheistic section comprises Cārvāka, Bauddha and Jaina.

Vaiśeṣika School

The Vaiśeṣika philosophy, no doubt, is the earliest systematic thought on the nature of the physical world. The *Vaiśeṣikasūtra* of Kaṇāda is the first systematic work on the laws of physical matters along with many other epistemological knowledge. Later works like the *Praśastapādabhāṣya* and its commentary the *Nyāyakandalī* of Śrīdhara, the *Kiraṇāvalī* of Udayana and many other works followed it.

All objects of experience can be classified into six categories:

dravya (substance), *guṇa* (quality), *karma* (motion), *sāmānya* (generality), *viśeṣa* (particularity) and *samavāya* (inherence). Later Vaiśeṣika (Śrīdhara, Udayana and Śivāditya) added one more category, *abhāva* (non-existence). The first three categories are defined as *artha* (which can be perceived) and they have real objective existence. The last three categories are defined as *buddhyapekṣa* (product of intellectual discrimination) and they are logical categories. Although the *Vaiśeṣikasūtra* of Kaṇāda has the six-category scheme of the *padārthas*, the seventh category *abhāva* is mentioned with its four varieties in the *Sūtra*.

DRAVYA (SUBSTANCE)

The nature of substance, qualities and motion has been elaborately studied. The substances are conceived as nine in number. They are: *pṛthivī* (earth), *ap* (water), *tejas* (fire), *vāyu* (air), *ākaśa* (ether), *kāla* (time), *dik* (space), *ātman* (self or soul) and *manas* (mind). The first five are called *bhūtas*, the substances having some specific qualities so that they could be perceived by one or the other external sense. The qualities residing in the substances have been mentioned. Important among these is the investigation to search for the cause of origination of the material universe. Going back, the Vaiśeṣika philosophy speculates the existence of the atoms at the end. According to the Vaiśeṣika school, the *tryaṇukas* (triad) are the smallest (perceivable) particles. These are made of three parts, each of which is defined as *dvyaṇuka* (dyad). The *dvyaṇukas* are conceived as made of two parts, each of which is defined as *paramāṇu* (atom). The *paramāṇus* (atoms) are indivisible and eternal, they can neither be created nor destroyed. Each *paramāṇu* possesses its own distinct *viśeṣa* (individuality).

GUṆA (QUALITY)

The *Vaiśeṣikasūtra* mentions seventeen *guṇas* (qualities), to which Praśastapāda added another seven. While a substance is capable of existing independently by itself, a *guṇa* (quality) cannot exist so. The original seventeen *guṇas* are: *rūpa* (colour), *rasa* (taste), *gandha* (smell), *sparśa* (touch), *saṅkhyā* (number), *parimāṇa* (size/dimension/quantity), *pṛthaktva* (individuality), *saṁyoga* (conjunction), *vibhāga* (disjunction), *paratva* (priority), *aparatva* (posteriority), *buddhi* (knowledge), *sukha* (pleasure), *duḥkha* (pain), *icchā* (desire), *dveṣa* (aversion) and *prayatna* (effort). To these Praśastapāda added *gurutva* (heaviness), *dravatva* (fluidity), *sneha* (viscosity), *dharma* (merit), *adharma* (demerit), *śabda* (sound) and *saṁskāra* (faculty). Apart from pleasure, pain, desire, aversion, effort and some others, the qualities like colour, taste, *saṁskāra* [velocity (*vega*), elasticity (*sthitisthāpaka*)] and sound are no doubt important qualities discussed in science. The propagation of sound has been investigated in the Vaiśeṣika philosophy. It is like the series of the water ripples. The *Nyāyakandalī* the commentary on the *Praśastapādabhāṣya* (ed. Durgadhar Jha, pp. 692-94), elaborates it: The sounds occupy successive points *ākāśa*. The first sound causes the second one. As soon as the latter is formed, the former gets destroyed. This kind of production and destruction goes on in a chain and what is perceived by the ear is the last of the series. When a drum is stuck by a stick the impact is believed to make vibrations as a consequence of which sound is produced in all directions. *Ākāśa* is the substratum of sound. The former is an eternal substance but the latter is a transient quality.

KARMA (MOTION)

There are five kinds of motions: upward movement (*utkṣepaṇa*), downward movement (*avakṣepaṇa*), contraction (*āikuñcana*), expansion (*prasāraṇa*) and locomotion (*gamana*).

THE VAIŚEṢIKA PHILOSOPHY INVESTIGATES THE CAUSE OF DIFFERENT TYPES OF MOTION

Weight (*gurutva*) is the non-inherent cause of the initial falling motion of a body. Fluidity (*dravatva*) is the non-inherent cause of flowing. A moving body possesses, at each moment in time, a particular "motion", which is to be thought of as a momentary, quality-like property of the body. "Motions" are defined to be the cause of conjunctions or disjunctions. A conjunction with a (stationary) body is brought about by displacement in space. We are thus to think of the motion of a body as being either identical with, or else the cause of, its displacement in space between two moments in time. A motion cannot be caused by another motion as that would lead to perpetual motion. A body is set in motion by its possession of a quality like "weight" or "fluidity". It persists in motion by having a dispositional property, "velocity" or "elasticity", which is the continuous cause of subsequent motions. It is brought to rest by coming into contact with other objects.

But answers to all the questions regarding motion are not got by the Vaiśeṣikas. The causes of the movement of an iron needle towards a magnet, the upward motion of flames, the movement of air and the initial motion of the atoms at the beginning of creation are not found out. They thought, there must be some "force" which initially gives rise to each of these motions, yet none of the "forces" so far isolated (weight/gravity, fluidity, elasticity) will do. The Vaiśeṣikas therefore speak of a new force, *adṛṣṭa* (the unseen force), alleged to account for such motions.

Thus, the Vaiśeṣika system has played an important role in the growth of the physical ideas in India. It had assumed a definite shape by the sixth century BCE. In the history of science, sixth century BCE has been regarded as the period which heralded the dawn of what has now come to be known as the Greek science. The Vaiśeṣika system contains in it the most important ideas on matter and motion, enunciated later by some of the leading Greek thinkers including Aristotle (from the beginning of the sixth century to the close of the fourth century BCE). Among the Greeks there were distinctly separate views and explanations of the knowable world. But there appeared no single system of the type of Vaiśeṣika among the Greek thinkers.

Yoga School of Indian Philosophy

Now I would like to come to the scientific thoughts in the Yoga philosophy. Yoga philosophy which prescribes the practice of *yoga*, i.e. controlling of the mental activities and physical movements, has been considered another source of scientific knowledge. It is amazing that *yoga* (physical and mental control) is considered as an important part of the medical treatment. *Yoga* is an ancient health science based on the experimental and experiential. The physical postures and meditative practices of *yoga* developed through thousands of years of intent study of the body's responses to particular postures and meditations. Many patients have already got on to *yoga* as a form of mental and physical self-care and preventive health. If we adequately understand *yoga*, we can have an opportunity to encourage the healthy thoughts and behaviours that our patients gain through *yoga* and to build upon them.

We the Indologists, having very scanty knowledge of the medical investigation in the *yoga* therapy, can only refer to the statement of the scientists in this field. So I would like to refer to the opinion and observation of Dr Timothy McCall, a board-certified internist and editor of the *Yoga Journal*. He in his article "Yoga as Medicine" lists forty research-supported ways that *yoga* heals. Research indicates that *yoga*'s benefits include increased flexibility, improved range of motion, strengthening of muscles and improvement in balance. These effects help prevent joint injuries and falls, and enhance endurance and coordination. *Yoga*'s breathing techniques, combined with cardiovascular exercises, actually improve lung function; studies show increased vital capacity and peak flow in individuals who regularly practise *yoga*. *Yoga* also improves posture, which makes more space for lung expansion. These two effects combined explain why *yoga* has been shown to decrease the need for medications in mild to moderate asthma. Furthermore, *yoga* teaches breathing through the nose instead of the mouth, which helps to filter pollen and pollutants that set off asthma attacks. Avoiding mouth breathing may also improve snoring and sleep apnoea.

Different schools of Indian philosophy have contributed to the scientific knowledge. We may identify the fields more and more where scientific ideas are embedded. The ancient seers of Indian philosophy observed the nature of outer world and inner mind and noted them. We can reinvestigate on their claims and reinstate the findings to showcase the glorious heritage of India. Thus the vague ideas will fade away and the young scholars will be respectful towards the society they live in.

9

The Asiatic Society and the Initiation of History of Science

Jagatpati Sarkar

SET up in 1784 The Asiatic Society is not only the oldest institution of Asia but also is a cultural icon of our country. Primarily a colonial construct, the vision of the founder Sir William Jones had a wide concept in building up the Society. The Society took interest not only in languages, literature and culture in the beginning, but also in the natural sciences as they were related to India. There was no idea of establishing a museum as a part of the Society's activities. But by 1796 it was found essential to erect a suitable building for housing antiquities of the Society. The Museum founded, developed under the care and guidance of Dr Nathaniel Wallich, a renowned botanist. The first three galleries like archaeology, zoology and geology were the starting point of the Museum of the Society. The science movement started from here. Actually when William Jones started his journey from England to India he noted down some important points to explore in India in which science was one of them. The points were:

1. The Laws of the Hindu and Mahomedans.
2. The History of the Ancient World.
3. Proofs and Illustrations of Scripture.
4. Traditions Concerning the Deluge, etc.
5. Modern Politics and Geography of Hindusthan.
6. Best Mode of Governing Bengal.
7. Arithmetic, Geometry and Mixed Sciences of Asiatics.
8. Medicine, Chemistry, Surgery and Anatomy of the Indians.

9. Natural Products of India.
10. Poetry, Rhetoric and Morality of Asia.
11. Music of the Eastern Nations.
12. The She-King or Soo Chinese Odes.
13. The Best Accounts of Tibet and Kashmir.
14. Trade, Manufacturing, Agriculture and Commerce of India.
15. Mughal Administration.
16. Maharatta Constitution.

One of the reasons why the Asiatic Society was eager to establish a museum was that by this time Englishmen had become aware of the cultural heritage of ancient India and of the importance of preserving and studying its remains. India had made known her progress in the physical science, especially astronomy, and it had drawn the attention of many Western scientists including Samuel Davis and John Playfair. Another English man keen of this study was William Hunter, who for sometime served as Secretary to the Society. During his stay in India, Hunter became interested in the Indian sciences and contributed seven papers to the *Asiatic Researches*. One of these was on the astronomical labours of Jaysimha, Rajah of Ambhere or Jayanagar. This provides the first detailed and scientific account of what are now known as Jantar Mantar, the unique astronomical structures built in the eighteenth` century by Astronomer statesman, Raja Sawai Jaisingh at Delhi, Mathura, Ujjain and Benares.

First of all the Europeans tried to explain the knowledge of science particularly Astronomy and Mathematics of India because they come aware that these two subjects are the mirror of civilization. The first European was Reuben Burrow who pointed out that the mathematical sciences were highly developed in ancient India. His paper on "A Proof that the Hindus Had the Binomial Theorem" was published in the second volume of the *Asiatic Researches* in 1804. He also tried to prove that although Newton was responsible for the application of the binomial theorem to fractional indices, the Hindus understood it in whole members to the full as well as Briggs and much better than Pascal.

Sir William Cecil Dampier once told:

> The vast and imposing structure of modern science is perhaps the greatest triumph of the human mind. But the story of its origin, its development and its achievements is one of the least known parts of history. This has hardly yet found its way into general literature. Historians treat of war, of politics, of economics, but of the growth of those activities has hardly been mentioned. These have revealed the individual atom and opened to our vision, the depths of space, etc. These have revolutionized philosophic thought and given us the means of advancing our material welfare to a level beyond the dreams of former ages. Most of them tell us little or nothing.

Gibbon believed that the best history could only be written by a historian philosopher, who distinguished those facts which dominate a system of relations.

Karl Marx once told:

> England has to fulfil a double mission in India: One destructive, the other regenerating — the annihilation of old Asiatic Society and the laying of the material foundation of Western Society in Asia. The Europeans founded the Asiatic Society at Calcutta in 1784.

Voltaire, for instance, in his *Ignorant Philosopher* remarks:

> It would be very singular that all nature, all the planets should obey eternal laws, and that there should be a little animal 5 feet high, who in contempt of these laws, could act as he pleased, solely according to his caprice.

An article on Hindu Astronomy by John Playfair is mentioned as being written in October 1792. This was received and published much later, in the 4th vol. of the *Asiatic Researches.* Jones had prefixed the 2nd vol. of the *Researches* with an "Advertisement" inviting learned European societies to transmit to the Secretary of the Asiatic Society in Bengal about a collection of short and precise queries on every branch of Asiatic History. He hoped that the society would gradually be able to provide answers to them which may prove in the highest degree beneficial to mankind.

John Playfair, Professor of Mathematics at Edinburgh, sent to the Society six questions with his own remarks on the development of the mathematical sciences in ancient India. Playfair was convinced that the Indians had in ancient times turned their attention to certain arithmetical investigations of which there was no trace in the writings of even the Greek scientist. He desired the society to find out if there were books on geometry and arithmetics in ancient India. He also suggested a complete translation of the *Sūrya Siddhānta*. He also suggested to draw up a catalogue of Sanskrit books on Indian Astronomy with a short account of each, and procuring descriptions of astronomical buildings and instruments of ancient India. He recommended that the skies should be studied together with an Indian astronomer to identify stars and constellations for which there were Sanskrit names. The *Sūrya Siddhānta* and a complete catalogue of Sanskrit MSS on Astronomy were published by the Asiatic Society, compiled by Professor A.K. Chakraborty in the year 2001.

The name of Bentley was also very popular in the history of the Society. He wrote an article "Antiquity of the Surya Siddhanta". Bentley read one of the most controversial articles in the history of the Society. J.D. Pearson attempted the scientific basis behind Hindu mythology and traditions. He also tried to explain the attributes of Śiva and presented an article in the *Asiatic Researches* in 1803. The most important paper of 1810 was an essay on the early history of Algebra, read by Edward Strachey on 3 October. He presented his observations in original, extent and importance of Mathematics among the ancient Hindus and from the Persian translations of the *Līlāvatī* and the *Bīja Gaṇita*. This paper traced the origin of the description of algebra to India as a landmark in this branch of study. Colebrooke acknowledged this contribution.

The Museum of the Asiatic Society possesses the priceless and unique collection of manuscripts, archival documents both in English and Russian, rare printed books, lithographs, paintings, busts, photograph prints, coins and copper plate inscriptions, etc. Works of art include an Edict of Emperor Aśoka on grey-granite stone in Brāhmī Script, *circa* 250 BCE Kharoṣṭhī Inscription of

Copper Plate of first century CE, etc.

A Tantra MS named the *Kubjikāmatam* in later Gupta script and a printed book on Astronomy published from Venice in 1497 are also in the Society's present collection.

Lastly, a cursory list of History of Science of the Asiatic Society publication is appended here. They are as follows:

1. *The Life and Works of Joseph Needham*, ed. Sushil K. Mukherjee and Amitabha Ghosh, 1997.
2. *The Endangered Earth,* A.P. Mitra.
3. *Subhankari*, Santanu Chakraborty.
4. *Studies in History of Sciences*, Santimoy Chatterjee, M.K. Dasgupta and Amitabha Ghosh, 1997.
5. *Rock Art Studies in India: A Historical Perspective,* Somnath Chakraborty.
6. *Rasarnava*, ed. Prafulla Ch. Roy, Harish Ch. Kaviratna, revised and annotated by Baini Prasad (Work No. 175, repr. 1985).
7. *Population Environment and Food Security,* M.S. Swaminathan.
8. *Porlarisation of Ionospherically Propagated Radio Waves*, S.R. Khastgir.
9. *Papers on Ayurvedic Studies*, ed. Brahmananda Gupta.
10. *Meghnad Saha in Parliament*, com. and ed. Santimoy Chatterjee and Jyotirmoy Gupta.
11. *Life and Experiences of a Bengali Chemist*, Prafulla Ch. Ray, vols I and II (repr. 1996).
12. *Krisi Parasara*, ed. and tr. Girija Prasanna Majumder and Suresh Ch. Banerjee, repr. 2001.
13. *History, Science and Society in the Indian Context*, ed. Arun K. Biswas.
14. *History of Indian Medicine Based on Vedic Literature: Śatapatha Brāhmaṇa,* Mridula Saha.
15. *Gopal Haider: Sanskritir Rasaraupadrasta*, ed. Sunil Behari Sensharma, Karunasindhu Das and Pallab Sengupta.

16. *Gleanings of the Past and the Science Movement,* A.K. Biswas.
17. *Gaṇitāvalī,* comp. Bibhuti Bhusan Bhattacarya, ed. Manabendu Banerjee and Pradip K. Majumder.
18. *Ganit Shastre Smaraniya Janra* (in Bengali), Pradip K. Majumder, vol. I in 1995.
19. *Father Eugene Lafont of St. Xavier's College, Kolkata and the Contemporary Science Movement,* Arun K. Biswas, 2001.
20. *Dawn of Modern Marine Science in India,* comp. and ed. Jyotirmoy Gupta.
21. *Collected Works of Mahendralal Sircar, Eugene Lafont and the Science Movement,* comp. and ed. Arun K. Biswas.
22. *Collected Works of Mahendralal Sircar, Eugene Lafont and the Science Movement,* comp. and ed. Saradindu Sekhar Ray.
23. *Collected Papers of Jnan Chandra Ghosh,* vols I and II.
24. *Bangla Bhasay Vijnan Charcha,* ed. Sarabindu Sekhar Ray.
25. *Aspects of History of Science,* ed. Naresh Ch. Dutta and Tulika Sen.

The Asiatic Society has been continuing its venture on the study of History of Science by publishing different articles in its journal and organizing regular workshops on History of Science till date.

10

Astronomical Manuscripts in Oriental Libraries of India

Ninth Century Onward

Somenath Chatterjee

INDIA has inherited a large number of manuscripts in Sanskrit literature which are not edited or read. Astronomical manuscripts are included in this category. Astronomical manuscripts are categorized as Siddhāntic, Karaṇa, eclipses and star charts. David Pingree concentrated on this field for future reference.

Introduction

Manuscripts are the product of intellectual activities of the past. Manuscripts inherited by a country are the identification on its intellectual past. India has inherited a large number of manuscripts on different subjects in Sanskrit, Persian and Arabic languages. In this paper only manuscripts of Sanskrit language are considered. The epics, Purāṇas and other texts are written in Sanskrit. *Mahārājās*, *rājās* and other rich men were the collectors of manuscripts. They appointed scholars or copiers to copy the manuscripts and preserved as their knowledge. Many scholars negotiated great distances to get a copy of the rare manuscripts. They deposited these MSS to libraries or stored in their own places. A large numbers of libraries were attached to the palace where manuscripts were preserved. Gift of a manuscript was considered highly meritorious.[1] There are instances of manuscripts being copied by great scholars like Pakṣadhara Miśra and Vidyāpati

[1] M.M. Anantalal Thakur, 2009, "Manuscriptology from Indian Sources", in *Aspects of Manuscriptology*, Kolkata: The Asiatic Society.

Thākur of Mithilā. Varāhamihira collected five astronomical manuscripts and compiled them as the *Pañcasiddhāntikā* which is the first manuscript compilation in India. Today, scholars of history of astronomy suggest that the Siddhāntic texts which are compiled by Varāhamihira are the first documents found in India. Āryabhaṭa, the pioneer of modern astronomy in India, applied mathematical theory to solve astronomical problems. Now, in different oriental libraries, the copies of *Āryabhaṭīyam* are available. To compile a concise history of astronomy in Indian context, it needs to edit almost all the manuscripts related to astronomy. H.T. Colebrooke, G. Thibaut, Sudhakar Dvivedi, Swāmi Vijñānānanda, David Pingree and many others tried to collect astronomical manuscripts and critically edited those works. M.M. Haraprasad compiled large amount of astronomical works in the Asiatic Society. David Pingree published a detailed bibliography of astronomical manuscripts. S.N. Sen compiled *A Bibliography of Sanskrit Works on Astronomy and Mathematics* in which details of astronomical works are included.

Two Latin words *manus* and *scriptus* are the origin of the word manuscript. According to the Antiques and Art Treasure Act 1972 of India "any manuscript is a hand-written composition, which has scientific, historical or aesthetic value and which has been in existence for not less than seventy-five years old". India has the oldest and largest collection of manuscripts that are to be preserved for next generation. The Constitution of India, under Fundamental Duties in Article 51A, states that "it shall be the duty to every citizen of India to value and preserve the rich heritage of our composite culture". In this paper, I would like to concentrate on astronomical manuscripts conserved in Oriental libraries.

We have a large number of astronomical manuscripts in Sanskrit language from eighth century onwards and those are given in Table 10.1.

M.M. Anantalal Thakur states that an Indian scholar's fond aspiration was to live among manuscripts. From the oldest times palm leaf was the major material for composing manuscripts. Birch bark was the next and the country-made paper began to be used from the twelfth century onwards. The oldest palm-leaf

Table 10.1: No. of Manuscripts on Astronomy during Eighth and Nineteenth Centuries CE

Era (Century CE)	*No. of MSS*
9	5
10	4
11	10
12	24
13	8
14	15
15	47
16	93
17	190
18	37
19	62
Undated	1,641
Total	2,136[2]

manuscript as known till now is the manuscript preserved in the Tokyo Museum (600 CE) and the manuscript on medicine which can be placed in the fifth century CE is on birch bark lying in the British Museum.[3] The oldest astronomical manuscript *Ṛk-Vedāṅga-Jyotiṣa* is found of 1370 BCE.

Importance of Astronomical Manuscripts

The glorious past of Indian astronomical knowledge lies in the manuscripts especially in Sanskrit manuscripts. These are the basic

---

[2] A. Rehman (ed.), 1982, *Science and Technology in Medieval India: A Bibliography of Source Materials in Sanskrit, Arabic and Persian*, New Delhi: Indian National Science Academy.

[3] Dilipkumar Kanjilal, 2009, "Manuscriptology", in *Aspects of Manuscriptology*, ed. Ratna Basu and Karunasindhu Das, p. 136, Kolkata: The Asiatic Society.

historical evidences which can truly say our history. These cover a variety of approaches to explain contemporary astronomical events. These manuscripts were the controller of the society. All religious rituals were obeyed through these writings. These survived manuscripts for centuries have significance of antiquity.

It is important to edit a text critically and for this reason manuscripts found in different zones are to be studied properly. The lines of every manuscript are straight and the letters are of same height.

samāni samapadāni samānasani samā śirāḥ ।
akṣarāṇi praṣṭhistavyāni mṛduni lalitāni ca ॥
— *Nandi Purāṇa*

When any manuscript is being copied, three methods are followed:

(a) Copying the text with notes.

(b) One *śloka* and its explanation.

(c) Copying the text in the middle portion of the page and writing notes in empty place.

Copy of astronomical manuscripts that are found mostly followed the first method, i.e. total copy of the text with notes.

The characteristics of manuscripts are equal in astronomical manuscripts like pagination, punctuation, abbreviation and colophon. The scribes of these manuscripts were well trained in astronomy and this lengthy toilwork was done only when they were passionate about it. Many works they copied stated *kaṣtena likhitaṁ grantha yatnena paripālayet*. Here is an appeal to conserve the manuscripts which are written with care.

In astronomical texts numbers are expressed by words, as one for moon (*candra*), *bhūmi*, *dharaṇī*, earth (*pṛthivī*), etc.; two for *yuga*, *netra* (eye), *bhujā* (arm), etc. A scholar of history of astronomy must learn how to read manuscript especially knowing word-numbers analogy.

In addition a scribe used to know that *aṅkasya vāmā gatiḥ* (numbers are counted from left side). From *Āryabhaṭīyam* (V.2):

vargākṣarāṇi varge 'varge 'vargākṣarāṇi kāt ṅmau yaḥ ।
khadvinavake svarā nava varge 'varge navāntyavarge vā ॥

> The *varga* letters (*ka* to *ma*) should be written in the *varga* places and the *avarga* letters (*ya* to *ha*) in the *avarga* places. '(The *varga* letters take the numerical values 1, 2, 3, etc.) from *ka* onwards; (the numerical value of the initial *avarga* letter) *ya* is equal to *ṅa* plus *m* (i.e. 5 + 25), the nine vowels should be written (one vowel in each pair of the *varga* and *avarga* places). In the *varga* (and *avarga*) places beyond (the places denoted by) the nine vowels too (assumed vowels or other symbols should be written, if necessary)'. —K.S. Shukla, *Āryabhatiya of Āryabhaṭa*

The Sanskrit alphabets are classified into five *vargas*; *ka-varga, ca-varga, ṭa-varga, ta-varga* and *pa-varga*. The letters are to bear numerical values 1 to 25 (Table 10.2).

The notational places are divided into the *varga* and *avarga* places. The odd places denoting unit's place, the hundred's place, the ten thousand's place and so on are called *varga* places and the even places denoting ten's place, the thousand's place, etc. are called *avarga* places.

The importance of astronomical manuscripts is to make our past astronomical knowledge open to the world.

Types of Sanskrit Astronomical Manuscripts

The astronomical works of India are divided mainly into two categories, viz.:

Table 10.2: Classification of Sanskrit Alphabets and Their Numerical Values

Varga	*Letters and Their Numerical Values*				
ka-varga	*ka* = 1	*kha* = 2	*ga* = 3	*gha* = 4	*ṅa* = 5
ca-varga	*ca* = 6	*cha* = 7	*ja* = 8	*jha* = 9	*na* =10
ṭa-varga	*ṭa* = 11	*ṭha* = 12	*ḍa* =13	*ḍha* = 14	*ṇa* = 15
ta-varga	*ta* = 16	*tha* = 17	*da* = 18	*dha* = 19	*na* = 20
pa-varga	*pa* = 21	*pha* = 22	*ba* = 23	*bha* = 24	*ma* = 25

The *avarga* letters *y* to *h* bear the following value:

ya = 30, *ra* = 40, *la* = 50, *va* = 60, *śa* = 70, *ṣa* = 80, *sa* = 90, *ha* = 100

1. Siddhānta treatises, and
2. Kāraṇa treatises.[4]

The *Sūryasiddhānta*, the *Āryabhaṭīyam*, the *Brahmasphuṭasiddhānta*, etc. belonged to the first category. Several Kāraṇas were written on the basis of the *Āryabhaṭīyam*. The *Kauṇḍakhyādaka* (the *kāraṇa* written by Brahmagupta), the *Kāraṇakutūhala* (written by Bhāskara), and the *Kāraṇaprakāśa* (written by Brahmadeva Gaṇaka) are the main Kāraṇa books of Indian astronomy.

Before the classic era, Jaina astronomical thoughts were known to scholars as the *Sūryaprajñapti* and the *Candraprajñapti*. These manuscripts have been studied carefully and their astronomical concepts were not accepted later. Five-years *yuga* system known from Vedāṅga-Jyotiṣa was continued up to the *Paitāmahasiddhānta*, which was the first Siddhāntic text in Indian astronomy. David Pingree in his *A Descriptive Catalog of the Sanskrit Astronomical Manuscript Preserved at the Mahārājā Sawai Mān Singh II Museum in Jaipur, India* categorized his findings as Siddhānta, Kāraṇa, Koṣṭha and eclipse. It can be assumed that he got the manuscripts separately and numbered in such a way. Another important classification of Indian astronomical manuscripts is: (a) divine, and (b) *pauruṣeya*. Divine means, in manuscripts, the name of the writer is absent. In manuscripts before Āryabhaṭa, writers' names are not found anywhere. Historians of astronomy assume the name from the next found anonymous manuscript. For example, in *Ṛk-Vedāṅga-Jyotiṣa*, no name is found. But in *Yajur-Vedāṅga-Jyotiṣa* the Sage Śeṣa noticed the name Lagadha as the writer of *Ṛk-Vedāṅga-Jyotiṣa*.

Āryabhaṭa was the first person who introduced himself in his book *Āryabhaṭīyam*. The contemporary astronomer, astrologer and mathematician Varāhamihira wrote his own name and location where he lived, so it is easier to locate the writer for future scholars.

Cataloguing of Manuscripts

---

[4] Bharadwaj, Sudhikant, 1991, *Sūryasiddhānta: An Astro-linguistic Study*, New Delhi: Parimal Publications.

DAVID PINGREE'S EDITION

Cataloguing of manuscripts has been initiated in last century by mostly individual effort. Satkari Mukhopadhyaya started an extensive survey of the cataloguing of manuscripts in 2006. From eighth to nineteenth century CE astronomical manuscripts of different materials are found. 1,641 manuscripts are found without name of writers and date (Table 10.1). Yet, according to linguistic logic, historians detect a period when these manuscripts were written.

Sawai Jai Singh II was an astronomy lover. He collected manuscripts and preserved them in his own library. Father of Swai Jai Singh II, Viṣṇu Singh paid close attention to the education of his son. He sent Jai Singh to Benares for his education. He received progress report of his son's education from *paṇḍit*s and also by his trusted servants. Jai Singh learned Sanskrit and Mathematics. When he was only thirteen years old he copied two astronomical manuscripts which are still preserved in Maharaja Swai Man Singh II Museum of Jaipur.

Jai Singh favoured Hindu astronomer Jagannātha Samrāṭ. The name of Jagannātha's father was Gaṇeśa. Jagannātha came in contact with the *rājā* at an early age. He was well versed in Sanskrit, Arabic and Persian languages as well as in Astronomy and Mathematics. When Sawai Jai Singh II initiated a vigorous programme in astronomical and mathematical works, Jagannātha translated the *Almagest* from Arabic to Sanskrit carefully. His approach and lucid style made the book popular. According to Jagannātha's version, the translation was done in a style so that even "a novice can comprehend its contents easily".[5] Jai Singh employed a number of competent scribes for coping manuscripts for his library. They copied the manuscripts in Sanskrit language using the Devanāgarī script. Among the vast astronomical activities of Jai Singh, collecting and copying works had a prime place. Maharaja Sawai Man Singh II Museum was founded in

---

[5] Sharma, Virendra Nath, 1995, *Sawai Jai Singh and His Astronomy*, Delhi: Motial Banarsidass.

1727 by Mahārājā Sawai Jai Singh II. With over 786[6] hand-written manuscripts the Pothīkhānā archives of the museum is regarded as one of the best in India. A majority of the manuscripts are hand-written copies of different subjects like medicine, astronomy, philosophy, religion and mathematical tables.

David Pingree compiled astronomical manuscripts with five scholars. It was published by American Philosophical Society, Philadelphia in 2003. They divided the catalogue into ten sections.

A. Vedic

B. Siddhānta

C. Kāraṇas

D. Koṣṭhakas

E. Eclipses

F. Star Charts

G. Geographical Tables

H. Astronomical Instruments

I. Translations

J. Miscellaneous

In the Preface of the book they said "there is a vast amount of unpublished manuscript material in Sanskrit, Arabic, Persian, and Latin, relevant to Mahārājā's activities".

The manuscripts belonging to the library of the Maharaja Sawai Man Singh II Museum, Jaipur are divided into four separate collections:

1. The Khāsmohor collection,
2. the Puṇḍarīka collection,
3. the Pothīkhānā collection, and
4. the Museum collection.

A few of the important astronomical manuscripts, which are

---

[6] David Pingree (ed.), 2003, *A Descriptive Catalogue of the Sanskrit Astronomical Manuscripts Preserved at the Maharaja Man Singh II Museum in Jaipur, India*, Philadelphia: American Philosophical Society.

listed in the book, are found in Khāsmohor:

- The *Āryabhaṭīyam*, Golādhyāya
- The *Āryasiddhānta*
- The *Bṛhaspatisiddhānta*
- The *Brahmatulyasāraṇī*
- The *Candrasūryagrahaṇādhikāra*
- The *Grahalāghava*
- The *Grahalāghavaṭīkā*
- The *Kāraṇakutūhala*
- The *Kāraṇaprakāśikā*
- The *Pitāmahasiddhānta*
- The *Siddhāntakaustubhamañjarī*
- The *Siddhāntasaṁhitāsāra*
- The *Siddhāntaśiromaṇi*
- The *Siddhāntaviveka*
- The *Sundarasiddhānta* (*Siddhāntasundara*?)
- The *Sūryasidddhānta*
- The *Tripraśnādhikāra*
- The *Vāsanabhāṣyapātādhyāya*
- The *Yantrarāja*
- The *Yantrarājaṭīkā*

Pingree and his associates did this tough job for future research. They separately listed the translation work, based on Islamic astronomy that Jai singh had acquired in the late 1720s. These are:

- The *Ukrā*
- The *Jarakīlīyantra*
- The *Yantrarājasyarasāla*
- The *Vakramārgavicāra*
- The *Lunar Tables of the Ulakabegījīca*

- The *Hayatagrantha*
- The *Siddhāntasindhu*
- The *Yantraprakāra.*

Pingree also categorized their works further to detect the category of manuscripts.

Siddhāntas

1. The *Paitāmahasiddhānta* from the *Viṣṇudharmottara Purāṇa*
2. The *Sūryasiddhāntasāravicāra*
3. Jagannātha's *Siddhāntakaustubha.*

Kāraṇas

1. A full version of the *Rājamṛgāṇka*
2. Dāmodara's *Sūryatulya.*

Koṣṭhakas

1. The unique manuscript of Moreśvara's *Markaṇḍaṭippaṇa*
2. The unique manuscript of Harinātha's *tithi, nakṣatra* and *yoga* tables
3. The unique manuscript of Goparāga's *Khagataraṅgiṇī.*

Eclipses

1. Observation and computations of lunar eclipses on 18 May 1761; 17 April 1772; 23 March 1773; 30 September 1773; 15 February 1775.

Star Charts

1. The star chart made by Mādhava Siṁha (1760 CE).

Geographical Tables

1. Two geographical tables.

Miscellaneous

1. Two manuscripts of Nandarāma Miśra's *Bhāgavata-jyotiḥśāstra bhūgolakhagolavirodhaparihāra.*

A few important astronomical manuscripts of Nāgarī script found in Oriental libraries are given in Table 10.3.

Table 10.3: Astronomical Manuscripts in Nāgarī Scripts in the Oriental Libraries

Works	*Details*	*Manuscript Found at*
Ābhiṣṭasāraṇī	Astronomical table	The Asiatic Society, Kolkata
Agaṇitacāra	Astronomical work containing a set of astronomical tables, yearly reckoner to calculate the movement of planets	Govt Oriental MSS Library, Madras (Chennai)
Āpastamba-Śulbasūtra	Containing 223 *sūtras* for the construction of sacrificial alters	1. Govt Sanskrit College Library, Benares 2. Viśva Bandhu, Hosiarpur
Āryabhaṭīyam	Works on mathematics and astronomy divided into four main parts	1. The Asiatic Society, Kolkata 2. University of Bombay, Mumbai (incomplete) 3. American Oriental Society, New Haven, CT 4. Calcutta Sanskrit College, Kolkata (incomplete) 5. Anup Sanskrit Library, Bikaner
Āryasiddhānta	Siddhāntic work containing 18 chapters	The Asiatic Society, Kolkata
Āryabhaṭa-sūtrādha-prakāśikā	Commentary on *Āryabhaṭīyam* of Āryabhaṭa I	1. The Asiatic Society, Kolkata 2. University of Bombay, Mumbai
Bakhśāli MSS (unknown)	It was written in birch bark. Seventy leaves of birch bark survived at the time of discovery.	Archaeological Survey of India, New Imperial Series, vol. 43, parts

Cont.

Table 3: *Cont.*

Works	*Details*	*Manuscript Found at*
	It is a mathematical work.	I-III.
Baudhāyana-Śulbasūtra (Bodhāyana)	It contains 525 *sūtras* and is divided into three chapters	The Asiatic Society, Kolkata
Baudhāyana-Śulbasūtravyākhyā (Dvārakānātha)	Commentary on the *Śulbasūtra* of Bodhāyana	Viśveśvarānanda Vedic Research Institute, MSS Collection, Hosiarpur
Bhāgpañcāṅga (Dvārakānātha)	Mathematical tables used for computing the calendar from a lunar time	British Museum, C. Bendall
Bṛhatsaṁhitāvivṛti Bhaṭṭotpala I (966 CE)	Commentary on the *Bṛhat Saṁhitā* of of Varāhamihira	Asiatic Society, Kolkata
Bhaumasāraṇī (Bhaṭṭotpala II) (1099 CE)	Astronomical table containing the motion of Mars	Panjab University Lahore, 2 vols
Bhāva-Nighaṇtu (Bhaṭṭotpala II) (1099 CE)	An anonymous astronomical work	Govt Oriental Manuscripts Library, Madras
Bhāvaprakāśa (Bhavāniśaṅkara)	An anonymous commentary on the *Āryabhaṭīyam* of Āryabhaṭa	Govt Oriental Manuscripts Library, Madras
Bhūgola (Bhūdhara Sūri) (1572 CE)	A description of the universe as found in the *Brahmāṇḍa Purāṇa*	1. British Museum 2. Bombay branch of the Royal Asiatic Society
Brahmasphuṭa-siddhānta (Brahmagupta) (*c.*628 CE)	Astronomical–mathematical work containing twenty-four chapters. This work influences the renaissance of Arab astronomy	1. Asiatic Society, Kolkata (Bengali) 2. Sanskrit College Library, Benares 3. University of Bombay, G.U. Devasthali 4. Viśveśvarānanda Vedic Research Institute, Viśva

Works	*Details*	*Manuscript Found at*
		Bandhu, Hosiarpur
Brahmasid-dhānta (*Śākalya Saṁhitā*) 821 CE (approx.)	Follows the *Sūryasiddhānta*, contemporary astronomical concepts are included	1. Asiatic Society, Kolkata 2. Sanskrit College Library, Benares 3. Calcutta Sanskrit College 4. Govt Oriental MSS Library, Madras
Brahmasiddhānta-sāraṇī	Astronomical work containing many tables	Panjab University Library, Punjab
Brahmasiddhānta (Viṣṇudharmotta-riya)	Part of the *Viṣṇudharmottara Purāṇa*	Sanskrit College Library, Benares
Brahmatulya siddhānta (Bhāskarācārya) (1183 CE)	A treatise of planetary motion	1. The Asiatic Society, Kolkata 2. Anup Sanskrit Library, Bikaner
Cakrayāsa (Cakradhara)	Astronomical work	Panjab University Library, Lahore
Candrasūrya-grahaṇa	An astronomical work for calculating the eclipses of the sun and the moon	Rajasthan Oriental Research Institute, Jodhpur
Chedyakopapatti	An astronomical work	The Bihar and Orissa Research Society, Patna
Dhruva-bhramaṇa lokavidhi (Nārmadīyakṛṣṇa)	An anonymous work	Udaipur
Dṛggṇita	Anonymous astronomical work dealing with rules of computation for compiling calendars from direct heavenly bodies	Govt Oriental MSS Library, Madras
Gaṇakaprakāśa (Ekanātha) (c.1600 CE)	A manual of astronomy containing nine chapters	Royal Asiatic Society, Bombay (Mumbai)

Cont.

Table 3: *Cont.*

Works	*Details*	*Manuscript Found at*
Dhrūvabhramaṇa-yantravyākhyā	A commentary on *Dhrūvabhramaṇayantra* of Padmanābha	Royal Asiatic Society, Bombay Branch
Gaṇasūyakoṣṭaka	Astronomical treatise	Private library in Gujarat
Grahalāghava	An astronomical work in 14 chapters	1. The Asiatic Society, Kolkata (incomplete) 2. Sanskrit College Library, Benares 3. CENSUS 4. Calcutta Sanskrit College (University)
Grahalāghava-vivṛti	A commentary of *Grahalāghava*	1. The Asiatic Society, Kolkata 2. Calcutta Sanskrit College (University)
Gaṇitaviṣaya	Astronomical work with tables and charts	Govt Oriental Manuscript Library, Chennai
Grahadarpaṇa	Astronomical work based on the *Sūryasiddhānta*	Durbar Library, Nepal
Grahasāraṇī	An astronomical work	Anup Sanskrit Library, Bikaner
Hayanagrantha	An astronomical work	Oudh
Jaiminisūtra	An astronomical work	The Asiatic Society, Kolkata
Jyotiṣasiddhānta Saṁgraha	A collection of astronomical works comprising the *Somasiddhānta*, the *Brahmasiddhānta*, the *Pitāmahasiddhānta* and the *Vṛddhavaśiṣṭhasiddhānta*	Printed edn available by Vindhyeśvarī Prasād Dvivedi
Jyotiṣasaṁgraha	An astronomical work	The Asiatic Society, Kolkata

Works	*Details*	*Manuscript Found at*
Jyotiṣasāra	An astronomical work	The Asiatic Society, Kolkata
Jyotiṣasiddhānta	An anonymous astronomical work	Mysore
Jyotiṣasūtra-vyākhyāna	An anonymous astronomical work	Mysore
Jyotpatti	An anonymous astronomical work	Oudh
Kālajñāna	An anonymous astronomical work	The Asiatic Society, Kolkata
Kararṇapaddhati (15 CE)	An astronomical treatise	Govt Oriental MSS Library Madras (Chennai)
Karaṇaprakāśa (1092 CE)	An astronomical work	1. Sanskrit College Library, Benares 2. University of Bombay
Siddhāntadarpaṇa	A short work on astronomy in 32 stanzas	Govt Oriental MSS Library, Madras (Chennai)
Siddhāntaśekhara	A Siddhāntic work on astronomy containing 20 chapters	1. Anup Sanskrit Library, Bikaner 2. Govt Oriental MSS Library, Madras (Chennai)
Siddhāntaśiromaṇi	An astronomical work 1. Gaṇitādhyāya 2. Golādhyāya	1. Anup Sanskrit Library, Bikaner 2. Calcutta Sanskrit College (University) 3. Oudh
Siddhāntatattva-viveka	An astronomical work	1. Calcutta Sanskrit College (University)
Somasiddhānta	An astronomical treatise following the *Sūryasiddhānta*, containing 10 chapters	1. Sanskrit College Library, Benares 2. Mysore

Cont.

Table 3: ***Cont.***

Works	*Details*	*Manuscript Found at*
		3. Tanjore Maharaja Serfoji's Sarasvati Mahal Library, Tanjore
Sphuṭanirṇaya-yantraḥ	An anonymous compendium of astronomical calculations in 6 chapters	Govt Oriental MSS Library, Madras (Chennai)
Sūrya-prajāpati	A Jain astronomical work. A descriptive catalogue of the Sanskrit Manuscript.	Asiatic Society, Kolkata
Sūryasiddhānta	A standard astronomical treatise contains 14 chapters	1. Asiatic Society, Kolkata 2. Sanskrit College Library, Benares 3. Bishop's College, Kolkata 4. India Office Library, London

Conclusion

It is very important to detect the astronomical manuscripts with the other ones existing in different Oriental libraries in India to get a clear history of astronomical knowledge of ancient and medieval India. An astronomer or a historian categorically makes his knowledge-base on his subject. He may or may not have expertise on languages like Sanskrit and Arabic. If a historian likes to read astronomical manuscripts written in Sanskrit then he should learn astronomy as well and Sanskrit. Our education system should be moulded in such a way that a student can read history, languages and science subjects simultaneously. It is the only solution to rediscover unread manuscripts on science subjects including astronomy.

Contributors

Amalendu Bandhyopadhyay, Professor and Senior Scientist, M.P. Birla Institute of Fundamental Research, Kolkata; formerly Director, Positional Astronomy Centre, Govt of India.

Dhirendranath Banerjee, formerly Secretary, Vangiya Sanskrit Siksha Parishad, Education Department, Govt of West Bengal.

Ramkrishna Bhattacharya, Fellow, Pavlov Institute, Kolkata.

Somenath Chatterjee, Individual Researcher.

Raghunath Ghosh, Professor Emeritus, Philosophy Department, University of North Bengal, Siliguri, West Bengal.

Dilip Kumar Mohanta, Professor, Dept of Philosophy, University of Calcutta; formerly Vice-Chancellor, Sanskrit College and University, Kolkata.

Parthasarathi Mukhopadhyay, Associate Professor, Dept of Mathematics, Narendrapur Rama Krishna Mission Residential College (Autonomous), Kolkata.

Sanjit Kumar Sadhukhan, Associate Professor, Rabindra Bharati University, Kolkata.

Jagatpati Sarkar, Senior Catologuer, Museum Section, The Asiatic Society, Kolkata.